ST. LOUIS GAMBLING KINGPINS

ST. LOUIS GAMBLING KINGPINS

JAMES R. DOYLE

THE
History
PRESS

Published by The History Press
Charleston, SC
www.historypress.com

Front cover images: *St. Louis Post-Dispatch*, June 18, 1944.
Back cover: Institute for Urban Research.

First published 2024

Manufactured in the United States

ISBN 9781467156226

Library of Congress Control Number: 2023949147

Notice: The information in this book is true and complete to the best of our knowledge. It is offered without guarantee on the part of the author or The History Press. The author and The History Press disclaim all liability in connection with the use of this book.

To Kathleen, for all the encouragement that made this possible in life and in spirit.

To Dad, for sharing the stories.

CONTENTS

CONTENTS

Gambling is a biological necessity....It will be legalized.

—James J. Carroll, in testimony before the Kefauver U.S. Senate hearings, 1951

ACKNOWLEDGEMENTS

Thanks to all my family members who offered words of wisdom and encouragement. Special thanks to fellow Doyle family members who had first review of drafts and thoughts and guidance: Terry, Vicki and Mike.

Thanks also to my first-read cousin, Mary Alice, for bearing the brunt of first passes in all the gyrations.

Thanks to Ancestry.com and Newspapers.com for their invaluable sources and research capabilities that guided this work.

Finally, thanks to all the kingpins who provided valuable inspiration for achievement.

INTRODUCTION

Here's the story.

Two of my dad's brothers, Uncle Vic and Uncle Jim, owned and operated a casino and handbook in the 1930s and 1940s. They became kingpins of betting. In other words, they were bookies and knew their way around a dice table. I learned from my dad's stories, from other elders and from what was written that in their day, these were respected individuals. They came to the city of East St. Louis, Illinois—or, as it was popularly referred to, the East Side—as children from a farm with their parents and other brothers and one sister.

Gambling was a wide-open operation in East St. Louis. The brothers became kingpins of betting by working their way from the stockyards and rolling cigars to become the owners and operators of the largest gambling casino in the Midwest.

They were not the only ones operating a dice game and a handbook. There were others who had good reputations themselves and were their own boss.

My uncles were from a strong Irish Catholic family and practiced their religion. One was a fourth-degree member of the Knights of Columbus. Both were married to, and living with, their first wives, and their children. Charities were blessed with their donations, and the two men helped others when it seemed the right thing to do. In reading stories from beyond the East Side and the Midwest, it seemed that gambling was sometimes considered evil and was constantly under threat of being made illegal.

But the general public seemed to enjoy the venues for gambling and participated where it was available.

My dad was a combat veteran of World War II and always said things were not the same on the East Side when he came back home. He was not happy with what he found. In my research for this book, it became clear how true that was. He was used to a booming city with casino and handbook operations with his brothers and their operating things from an independent ownership basis.

He was greeted on his return by the casino participating in payoff arrangements to maintain safety at the venue and the intrusion of organized crime into the bookmaking business. At the same time, the composition of the city was changing. One of his brothers had passed away while he was gone. The other brother eventually decided to step away from operating things due to the criminal intrusions. Dad went on to different ventures himself.

It got me thinking about whether there were similar individuals who were well respected and operated within the betting industry at the same time. While gaming has changed since my uncles' days, that entrepreneurial spirit and drive still exists throughout the United States.

My thought was that a look at the uncles and a select group of contemporaries could benefit myself and others and offer insight into what they did and how it turned out. Hopefully, it would also show us how to achieve and maintain that entrepreneurial drive in today's business climate.

When looking at a draft of this book, an associate was astounded that I was treating bookmakers as legitimate businesspeople. That's the point. They were bookmakers, and some thought them improper—evidently, my associate among them. A significant number of individuals have felt that, as in the United Kingdom and Las Vegas today, casino owners and bookmakers are considered honorable professions.

I went on the search for past kingpins and found sixteen individuals whom I considered close matches to my uncles. Gangsters and organized criminals did not qualify. It required a search covering fifty years to find individuals who would stand out as independent business operators in betting, especially in the odds-making and bookmaking fields.

To research this required an examination of what and where gambling stood in the period from 1900 to 1950. It became clear that horse racing and all its factors would dominate the list of that time.

It was considered best to look not only at how individuals and gambling changed from 1900 to 1950, but also where we are today. The changes from 1950 to 2023 were also considered to bring a current view to the landscape that had been laid by these sixteen kingpins. They were the entrepreneurs of yesteryear. Today, we also have entrepreneurs and kingpins, but their focus is different, directed at other industries. Gambling is still open, but it has become a large-scale business, not one dominated by individuals.

One significant impact from these changes between 1900 and 1950 was that organized crime became an increasing force. Crime operations became even more dominant from 1950 to the 1970s. Starting in the 1960s, with the investor Howard Hughes, others were able to gain a foothold in the state of Nevada and the city of Las Vegas. The eventual upshot of this was that organized business was able to overthrow organized crime and gain its own dominance over the revenues from the largest single source of legal gambling.

In the first half of the twentieth century, a certain type of person gravitated to gambling. Gambling involved dice, roulette, blackjack and poker, but horse racing stood out as the dominant betting form. The sport had always involved betting, and a bookmaker being involved in the outcome was a common practice. In several instances, bookmakers rose to be kingpins. They became nationally known for their odds-making in horse racing and in others sports at the time, including prizefighting, baseball and football. Oddsmakers also had a strong preference for betting on presidential races.

The composition of the bets and method for placing them have changed considerably over time, but the sports involved remain consistent. The level of play on the field has changed, but the sports themselves are all still in play when it comes to betting. Football, basketball, baseball, horse racing and ice hockey are still in play. Bets can also be made on pastimes that tend to draw smaller audiences, including cricket, rugby and American soccer.

One change from past betting patterns is that horse racing is no longer the dominant industry it was in the period I cover in this book. It still draws considerable betting action, but not at the premier level.

Football is clearly the dominant and most popular sport in the United States today. It draws the overwhelming share of betting wagers for both the college and professional seasons.

Betting is still increasing, and the bookies are still in play. Hopefully, this book can serve as a helpful guide for future entrepreneurs in their quest to become kingpins of a new industry.

1

GAMBLING IN AMERICA

GAMBLING DIRECTION

From 1900 to 1950, there was a tremendous growth in gambling in general and sports betting in particular. We're going to profile those individuals who gained prominence at this time. These entrepreneurs applied their skills to become casino owners, handbook operators and what is known today as information service providers. They became "gambling kingpins" and helped establish the success enjoyed by today's gaming industry.

Gambling has changed over time to a degree not seen in other industries. Namely, it has gone back and forth between being legal and illegal, operating under different local political enforcement rules and in the shadow of organized crime. There have also been shifting federal guidelines and directions.

Betting in the United States has taken on a new life and direction from its existence in the past. Casinos and sports betting are now legal in most states. Looking at the history of betting in the country can shed light on how this was made possible, even when it operated in a completely different environment.

Today, casino gambling has expanded to multiple states and to Native American lands.

Finding an individual gambling kingpin in 2023 is difficult. Most new casinos and bookmaking operations have been started by organizations composed of publicly owned companies, shareholders or groups of investors.

The spirit of entrepreneurship with the desire for independence, individual ownership and financial success is alive and well today. Jeff Bezos, Elon Musk and Bernard Arnault represent the modern kingpins but participate in different industries, not gambling.

BOOKMAKERS

A bookmaker, also known as a bookie, is a person or company that accepts bets on sporting events and other activities at agreed-on odds. Bookies set the fixed odds at horse-race tracks in 1900. They were actually at the track, in designated areas. Today, you can still walk up to a bookie at a track or casino or use your technology of choice to contact them to place a bet.

These pioneering individual bookmakers and gambling operators saw their rise and fall happen between 1900 and 1950. There are no specific dates for the beginning and end of this era. Generally, this period hit its stride in the major cities while these areas were seeing significant growth and development. Gambling activity was overseen on a state-by-state basis.

Its decline didn't end at a specific date, but 1950 is when the federal government began a determined effort to make gambling illegal, a result of the encroachment and influence of organized crime across state boundaries.

Over the decades, bookmaking, depending on the location, has operated in the open both legally and illegally, including underground operations. Many a politician and police force ensured the open operation, as well as making sure it went underground when necessary. As today with pioneer Las Vegas investors Sheldon Addelson and Steve Wynn, political involvement and contributions were a must, regardless of time or political party.

Bookmakers had a positive status in many communities. Some individuals looked at bookmaking as the tech industry of its day, offering opportunities for personal and financial success. Some bookies rose to high levels and then went on to other major kingpin ventures. A good number moved into real estate; others invested in professional sports teams.

Recent changes in public policy have made it possible to have sports betting in states where it is authorized. In other words, it is now legal to have bookmakers operate and to do so in the open. There has been an exponential growth in the number of states that allow bookmakers. By

2023, bookmakers have gone from primarily individuals to mostly large organizations with boards of directors and investors.

Gambling Choice

In the days before 1900, the major kingpins were men like Andrew Carnagie, Cornelius Vanderbilt and J.P. Morgan, and the entrepreneurial opportunities were in railroads, steel, stockyards and banks.

The 1900 seeker of financial independence did not enjoy this foundation, nor did they have the Internet as an outlet for entrepreneurial opportunity. But they still had the chance to be entrepreneurs if they possessed a desire to seek possibilities of achieving financial success. The mathematical whizzes of those days could be found in handbooks and casinos.

There was one area of entrepreneurial opportunity that any individual could enter with the necessary skills and determination: gambling. The opportunity to be a professional gambler primarily involved table games. The more favorable schemes for the mathematically inclined were in betting and bookmaking. Specifically, these skills were applied to the increasingly popular sport of horse racing. Many places around the country offered handbooks and bookmakers. There were other opportunities to host casino-type games, and many places operated them along with handbooks at different levels. Individual bookmakers in this period offered the greater opportunity to become self-made and wealthy. These opportunities blossomed in the major cities, which were undergoing population and employment growth. This fueled the ability and desire for working individuals to gamble and increase their wealth as a supplement to a paycheck.

The gambling industry provided entry for individuals and opportunity to forge a success at an honest table game of poker or blackjack or a roll at the dice table. Just like the tech independents of 2023, they were faced with satisfying government regulators. Instead of the Securities and Exchange Commission's reporting requirements, the bookmakers had state and local government officials to keep happy. At this time, it wasn't the U.S. Department of Justice that had to be contended with, but the local police forces.

Regardless of oversight, the opportunity for immediate failure with an ill-advised bet was also present. The bookmakers didn't have venture capital founders. They needed to have a bankroll for their handbook to sustain itself. They had to know how to work with luck and chance and utilize mathematical skills regarding probable successful outcomes. There was no board of directors to monitor them, only finical outlook projections for success. Instead, bookmakers had customers placing bets at odds determined by bookmakers in the hopes they were successful in their choices. Table games were monitored by the same board of bettors. The owner of the games had to be successful and honest. The likelihood of a board's disapproval would be apparent immediately, and not in the somewhat civilized manner of modern times.

Political Directives

To top it all off was the fact that gambling was both legal and illegal in different states at different times. Regardless of the legislative directive at any given place or time, gambling continued.

Gambling has been a debated issue in the United States since Revolutionary War days. To make gambling legal or to prohibit it was a political issue, a criminal issue, a wealth issue and an operational issue. It is a question that has been pondered by preachers, politicians, cities, states and the country.

There is an adage: Don't pass a law that you know can't be enforced. The country has taken a long time to understand this notion. The national alcohol prohibition of the 1920s and the public reaction against it must be a lesson to lawmakers today. The legal status of gambling has taken a longer and more circuitous journey than did that of alcohol.

There have been several gambling approach and avoidance laws passed in the United States. Between 1900 and 1950, political cooperation was a must for gambling to continue, which included bookmaking at different times and places. Of course, this included police cooperation. Political contributions by gambling interests were a given.

By 1950, anti-gambling legislation reached a crescendo in a variety of states and at the national level. Nothing immediately resulted, but it began a change that has brought full-functioning casinos and bookies operating with state approval in most states. Changes in population growth and location as well as the influence of organized crime served to put a damper on bookmaking and casino operations that had grown during the 1900–50 period. Major shifts during this time brought about the demise of the individual entrepreneurial kingpin.

Recent years have seen an abundance of positive gambling legislation, including allowing sports betting in a significant number of states. This legislation focuses on the creation and operation of sports betting. In other words, bookmakers have been made legal. This approval is for both a physical location as well as betting via a tech device of an individual's choice within the state of approval.

2

GAMBLING ECONOMICS

POPULATION GROWTH

In 1900, there were seventy-six million people in the United States, and that number was growing each day. New York, Chicago, Philadelphia and St. Louis were, in that order, the four largest cities in the country. In 1910, that stayed the same, with each city experiencing growth in population and industry. New York, Chicago, Philadelphia and St. Louis were the dominant cities of the day.

As the population expanded, jobs were created, workers were hired and new businesses opened. Workers had money to spend. Gambling was an American pastime that entrepreneurial bookmakers saw had the potential for expansion.

The city areas being looked at still exist today, but not all are at the level and texture they possessed in the past.

CITY INFLUENCES

The four largest U.S. cities in 1900 have undergone changes since that year. New York and Chicago are still in the top four, but Philadelphia and St. Louis have moved down from their height. Since 1900, St. Louis has played a major local and regional role in betting with bookmakers and at the creation of casinos, all in the context of national changes.

Surprising as it may seem today, St. Louis in 1900 was a western boomtown, much like Los Angeles became and, to some extent, Phoenix is today. It showed its position by hosting the Olympics and a world's fair in 1904. It was the "Gateway to the West" and has the Gateway Arch sticking out of the ground to show it.

It was a booming city and possessed all the qualities that entails, from business expansion and new immigration to wealth creation, expanding housing and population and a demand for public and private services.

Bookmakers and casinos were in full force at this time. St. Louis began on the banks of the Mississippi River. Directly across the river is the Illinois town of East St. Louis, which became known as the "East Side." This area grew to become a more vital bookmaking and casino operation than St. Louis. East St. Louis represented only a small portion of metropolitan St. Louis's population, but gambling was a basic economic resource and integral part of East St. Louis's fabric. Handbooks, table games and slot machines could be found throughout the city, and they flourished in a generally wide-open way and had a major impact on St. Louis.

New York has a similar geographic situation, being located across the Hudson River from New Jersey. But, unlike the case with St. Louis, New York, particularly the borough of Manhattan, dominates the region. Chicago was different, lacking a bordering river. It adjoins Wisconsin and Indiana and is clearly the dominant city in the region. Its influence, however, is split between the North and South Sides of the city. Philadelphia, like New York, was adjacent to New Jersey. In its case, Gloucester City in New Jersey and Atlantic City had significant impacts on its gambling opportunities.

Regardless of city, gambling operations were overseen by independent, individual operators, and their operations laid the groundwork for betting as we know it today.

Gambling Growth

The period between 1900 and 1950 was an exhilarating one in the United States. There are issues from this time that continue today regarding betting with bookies and casinos.

That era was a transformative one for gambling in the United States. A lot has changed in the nation and the world. Economic and cultural impacts were felt by cities and communities from coast to coast. Our focus will be on the changes and activities in the betting world, but most importantly we'll be looking at the "betting kingpins" who oversaw and influenced gambling during this time.

Gambling at this time was a flourishing economic and political force. Was it legal? The laws at the time said no. The general public said yes. At least, that was their preference. And regardless of location, they participated as if it was legal.

Gambling was overseen by the states. There was no federal dictate at this time. The effects of federal involvement were felt most intensely starting around 1950. The federal government's involvement created a bevy of changes that tended to diminish gambling in the United States. We're not going to explore all the changes that resulted from the federal government's influence, but we'll look at what happened to the betting kingpins between 1900 and 1950 that contributed to federal involvement.

During this period, it took a combination of political acquiescence, police cooperation and the strong-willed nature of independent operators to maintain and run a successful handbook or casino operation.

Gambling Choices

Gambling has been a part of the United States since the country began. After the American Revolution, French settlers introduced table games like roulette, and these continue today. Craps was first played on boats, in saloons and in cotton fields in the United States around 1800. In 1827, the first twenty-four-hour, full-service casino opened in New Orleans.

Lotteries were active in Revolutionary War days but were banned throughout the country in 1830. The ban wasn't lifted until 1960. From 1835 to 1851, multiple states passed laws banning gambling. By 1858, even though still not legal, Mississippi riverboat gambling started gaining popularity. Poker was a popular table game at the time and became famous in the Wild West days of Wild Bill Hickok

Gambling in 1900 consisted of betting on a variety of things and playing a variety of games. Horse racing, baseball, billiards, golf and tennis were favorites to bet on. Prizefights and political voting joined that list. Lottery games and numbers were also popular.

In 1910, blackjack, or twenty-one, was first played in Evansville, Indiana. It became the most significant game by revenue in the nation by 2020. In 1905, the first true slot machine had arrived, and by 1915, camouflaged slot machines started to appear.

Casino betting focused on dice, blackjack, poker and roulette.

3

GAMBLING

1900s-1920s

HORSE RACING

Gambling between 1900 and 1950 consisted of betting on a variety of activities. One sport rose above the rest in popularity. Horse racing became the dominant sports betting activity in the United States.

The sports bettor needed a facilitator to make the bets and receive returns if they won. These individuals became known as bookmakers, and where they operated changed from city to city. Their legal status also varied. They became a major force in sports betting in general and in horse-race betting in particular.

Horse racing as a spectator and betting sport can be traced to the Roman Empire. It found its way to America at the start of the country. By 1890, there were 314 racetracks in the United States, operating in nearly every state. Freehold Raceway in New Jersey is the oldest racetrack in the nation, with formal horse racing beginning in 1854. Monmouth Park Racetrack opened for harness racing in 1870. But by 1894, the New Jersey legislature had banned pari-mutuel betting as well as all types of gambling, essentially shutting down the racetracks.

Racetrack regulation was overseen by the states, and their operation was somewhat different than it is today. The racetracks were generally owned by an individual or a small group of individuals. There were multiple tracks within a given community. A significant difference was the lack of a starting gate. Even more relevant to our look at gambling kingpins

Above: St. Louis Fairgrounds and Horse Racecourse in 1874. It closed in 1905. No other tracks have since opened in Missouri. *Missouri History Museum.*

Left: Running of the 2007 Breeders Cup Classic at Monmouth Racetrack in New Jersey. The track began in 1870 and has continued operations into 2023. *awesomgemfirstturn.jpg. Breeders.com.*

was the inclusion of bookmakers. Betting on the races was performed by bookmakers at the tracks.

In those days, bookies were located at each of the tracks and placed within a designated area, where they were allowed to operate and accept bets at odds established by the bookies and pay out if a bettor won. Betting at tracks became a major issue of protest by the anti-gambling crowd.

Anti-gambling legislation varied from state to state, but the essence was that betting at tracks began to be prohibited, and this effectively served to close down the tracks.

St. Louis South Side Racetrack was the first in the United States to offer electric lights for racing. For winter racing, it offered a glass enclosure. It closed in 1905. *Drawing from St. Louis Globe-Democrat, February 8, 1920.*

In 1905, St. Louis was known for its racetracks. The first big one was found at the North Side Fairgrounds Park. This was privately owned but sold to the City of St. Louis in 1902 so that it could participate in the upcoming 1904 World's Fair. This was closely followed by the 1902 opening of Sportsman's Park, also on the North Side. Another track was known as the South Side Track, and in the middle of the city was Delmar Track. The East Side had two tracks: the East Side Track in East St. Louis and the Madison Track north of East St. Louis in Madison, Illinois. Both cities had bridge access across the Mississippi River from St. Louis.

A key feature in the 1890s and early 1900s in New York, Chicago and St. Louis was that they had multiple tracks. The small population base in St. Louis and on the East Side had five in operation at the time, with all drawing good crowds.

Besides joining in the national trend of racetrack proliferation, the St. Louis and East Side tracks also introduced features not found at other tracks. The primary innovations were the introduction of winter and nighttime racing. The accompanying picture doesn't quite show it, but stoves were placed around the track area to help keep spectators warm behind a glass enclosure. The artificial illumination was evidently quite glaring, but that didn't stop racing enthusiasts from attending, regardless of time or weather.

The heating and lighting innovations continued until the reform movement hit Missouri and the tracks were closed. At the same time, Illinois passed similar legislation, and the Madison and East St. Louis tracks closed around 1905.

Beginning in 1905, daytime racing was the primary form of horse racing. It took a while before night racing was tried again. When it did, the 1900-era illumination was improved and placed at several tracks. Cold weather racing today involves more than just a stove to keep spectators warm.

Anti-gambling groups have existed since gambling began, and the approaches to making the activity illegal—and the methods to avoid these prohibitions—have taken on a variety of forms. The United States in 1908 saw the anti-gambling crowd on the winning side, eliminating a majority of the 314 racetracks, taking their number down to about 25 in operation.

New York's legislature declared illegal the making of odds and receiving funds at a fixed place—that is, having bookmakers and betting taking place at the track. As a result, there were no more racetracks in New York in 1911. They returned in 1913 with legalized pari-mutuel betting, and this then occurred in other states. This move allowed racetracks to reopen.

Pari-mutuel betting provides for pool betting, with odds and payouts determined by the pool of bettors placing bets at tracks. This didn't make bookmakers disappear; it only made them provide different odds and payouts away from the tracks.

In 1904 in the State of Missouri and in the City of St. Louis, a new slate of anti-gambling politicians was elected. They managed to eliminate all St. Louis racetracks by 1905. No horse race tracks have appeared in the state or city since that time.

In keeping with this trend, Illinois passed similar legislation, which had the effect of closing down the Madison and East Side tracks, along with those in Chicago. The East Side Track was owned by two brothers who were both bookmakers, Joe and Cole Ullman. They closed the track down and went back to Chicago, where they also had an interest in racetracks. After the Illinois legislation was passed, the East Side Track closed. Joe passed away in 1908, and Cole stayed in Chicago. Illinois had a different outlook from Missouri, and Chicago saw stops and starts trying to get tracks back in business, with limited success.

This is the grandstand at Fairmont Park Racetrack, on the East Side, 2023. The track opened in 1925. It was the first track in the St. Louis area since 1905. *Fairmont Park. fairmontpark.com.*

It took until 1925 for a racetrack to return to the St. Louis area. The East Side community of Collinsville saw the opening of Fairmont Park's track. It is in proximity to East St. Louis and continues operating to this day. It remains the only racetrack in the greater St. Louis area. Ownership has changed several times over the years. In 2000, ownership passed to William Stiriz, chairman of Ralston Purina at the time. He is now retired from the company and still owns the track.

The Corrigan family opened the Hawthorne Racecourse in 1891 and closed it in 1905. They sold it to Thomas Carey in 1909. The Corrigan family sold it to try a short meet in 1916, but then it closed down until reopening legally in 1922. It has been in operation since then in various forms and still involves the Carey family.

DAILY RACING FORM

As a result of the increasing interest in horse racing, a publishing kingpin was created.

The story related by John Wray, longtime sports columnist for the *St. Louis Post-Dispatch*, is that in his early days, he was credited with devising the past-performance chart, which became the backbone of success of horse racing. He developed this with a fellow *Post* worker at the time who was working on Louis Cella's *St. Louis Racing Form*. When the 1905 reform outlawed racing, the *Racing Form* folded.

A different attitude in regard to Illinois legislation was Frank Brunell's gain. Frank was in Chicago, and on November 17, 1894, he created the *Daily Racing Form* and published a four-page broadsheet. By 1896, the *Daily Racing Form* had published its first chart book. Around the same time as John Wray's innovation in 1905, Brunell was revolutionizing horse betting by his belief that a horse's past performance was a major factor in determining future performance, and he published a past-performance record for each horse in a race. Within a few months, Brunnell had copyrighted the idea. The *Daily Racing Form* continues in 2024 as the only daily national newspaper dedicated to a single sport.

The publication has seen several ownership changes over the decades, from an individual owner to presently being part of an LLC private-equity company. But it continues to publish every day except Christmas, with as many as twenty-five daily editions.

4

LOUIS CELLA

HORSE TRACK KINGPIN

A true multiple kingpin of horse racing during this period was Louis Cella of St. Louis. In the late 1890s and early 1900s, horse racetracks were in flux, but Louis was securing and operating all the racetracks he could purchase. He became a multiple kingpin in his day.

Cella's parents immigrated to St. Louis from northern Italy. Louis was born in 1866 in downtown St. Louis. His four brothers were also born there. He went to work as a boy to help support the family. Louis went off to Kansas City for a time to be a bartender and then returned to St. Louis and opened a saloon downtown. It became known for its dice games, and Louis made a large sum from its operation.

Taking these funds, he joined up with Texas Tom Walsh in St. Louis, and together they went to the East Side, to Madison, located just across the Mississippi from North St. Louis. In 1895, they also operated the Monte Carlo gambling house and separate bookmaking sites. They then purchased a minority interest in the Madison track and owned a string of horses. The Madison location was in proximity to the North St. Louis Fairgrounds Park track. This privately owned operation was sold to the City of St. Louis in 1902 to make it available for the upcoming world's fair. Louis then went to the nearby Sportsman's Park and turned it into a racetrack; he had it closed in 1905.

Louis got his start by operating a saloon and craps tables. Based on his winnings, he switched to bookmaking, while at the same time owning and racing horses. In 1896, he formed with fellow St. Louisans Samuel Adler and Cap Tilles a partnership in the United States known as CAT.

LOUIS CELLA.

Louis Cella is shown here in 1905. Cella's investment syndicate-controlled St. Louis racetracks and twenty-five other U.S. tracks. From 1897 to 1904, his group had a monopoly on horse racing in the Midwest. Spokane Press, *June 7, 1905.*

The partnership dominated the Midwest horse-racing industry through World War I. The group founded the Western Turf Association, which granted Cella and his group nearly monopolistic control over jockeys, bookmakers and horse owners in the Midwest.

At the same time, Louis maintained his saloon in St. Louis. In 1895, he ran as a Democrat for a statehouse seat. He lost but maintained an active interest in politics and political donations.

Louis ended his relationship with Walsh and went on to start CAT, which proceeded to purchase a full interest in the Madison track in Illinois. From that beginning, the group controlled St. Louis racing by purchasing Sportsman's Park as a racetrack in 1902, along with controlling Delmar Racetrack and South Side Racetrack. The St. Louis tracks were closed in 1905. By 1911, the CAT group's Western Turf Association had purchased tracks in Nashville and Memphis, Tennessee; Little Rock and Hot Springs, Arkansas; New Orleans, Louisiana; Detroit, Michigan; Cincinnati, Ohio; Latonia and Louisville, Kentucky; and Fort Erie, Ontario.

In 1905, Louis closed the St. Louis tracks. Blind John Condon, the owner of racetracks in Chicago, also had to close his tracks. Condon, along with Dan Stuart of the Fort Erie Racetrack, had previously joined to purchase the Oak Lawn Track in Hot Springs Arkansas.

Louis, with his brother Charles, joined in the purchase of an interest in Oak Lawn alongside Condon and Stuart. Louis and Charles also joined Condon and Stuart in the purchase of the Fort Erie track.

The Fort Erie track in Canada, located near Buffalo, New York, did not encounter the issues found in America. The racetrack stayed in the Cella family until it was sold in 1952. Fort Erie remains in operation as a major Canadian horse-race facility. At Oak Lawn, races were held only in 1906 and 1907, when the anti-gambling group won again and racing was suspended until 1916. Both Condon and Stuart had passed away by this time; the Cella brothers gained control. When Louis died in 1918, full control of the track went to Charles. Racing was suspended again in 1919 and stayed that way

Pari-mutuel board and track in 2013 at Oak Lawn in Hot Springs, Arkansas. Louis Cella and his brother purchased this track in 1916. Members of the Cella family continue its operation. *Oak Lawn. oaklawn.com.*

until 1934. The Hot Springs track remained in Charles's family and was still operating in 2023.

Louis took his proceeds and invested in real estate in St. Louis, where he owned five theaters, an office building and a hotel, as well as the shuttered racetracks and other purchased tracks. He died at the relatively young age of fifty-one in 1918. He left behind an estate estimated to be worth $10 million (about $1 billion in today's terms).

5

BARNEY SCHREIBER

TURF MAN

Around the same time that Louis Cella was active, another St. Louis–based kingpin was operating.

Barney Schreiber led the way in horse-race betting. He was a German immigrant who found his way to the United States and wound up owning, breeding and racing horses and making book on them.

He was a bookmaker in the different races at the tracks of his day. He laid the foundation for betting on modern horse racing and mentored other bookmakers to huge success. Barney was a true kingpin.

The horse-racing tracks of Barney's day had bookmakers at the track quoting fixed odds and paying off when appropriate.

Barney began his quest in the 1890s. Around 1891, he started as a clerk in a men's furnishing store in Kansas City. He went to St. Louis's South Side Racetrack around 1893 and placed bets for the Doyle Company of Kansas City. Observing that the bookies got most of the profits, he decided to join their ranks. Barney began a partnership operating a book under the name of Doyle and Company and made enough at the East Side Track to start as the owner of a string of horses after a year. He also found a top jockey named Felix Carr, who consistently won for Barney. Barney's string of horses and his jockey traveled to Chicago and made a fortune.

Over the next three years he took the money from betting and purchased a breeding farm in an area just outside the St. Louis city limits. Eventually, he created the Woodlands breeding farm and after a few years was raising more horses than anyone in the West.

y Schreiber and Finish of $10,000

Left: Barney Schreiber was known as the man who distinguished himself by turning a $20 bet into $1 million in winnings. He became the best-known turf man in the West and owed his fortune to the St. Louis tracks of his day. St. Louis Post-Dispatch, *December 12, 1909.*

Right: Barney Schreiber's horse Jack Atkin, shown winning a 1910 race by a nose at the Dominion Handicap at the track in Fort Erie. The $10,000 prize equates to $2 million in 2023. Buffalo Courrier, *1910.*

Because of the 1905 Missouri and Illinois track closures, Barney went to tracks that were still operating. In 1906, Kentucky formally legalized the pari-mutuel horse-racing betting system; New York and Maryland followed soon after. Throughout the twentieth century, other states followed Kentucky. In 2023, forty states had defined racing jurisdictions and allowed pari-mutuel betting. Essentially, the bookmakers didn't need to be at each track and quote odds in person. Contrary to the pari-mutuel at tracks, bookmakers offered fixed-odds betting with a payout known in advance and better odds than at the track.

Some of Barney's horses were famous in their day and won large sums. Prominent among them were the progeny of Sain, a famous sire. Other famous horses were Good Hope, Don Carille Bannockburn, Lacy Crawford, Dr. Gardner and Tom McGrath. Barney became owner of the noted stallion Sain, and other great horses under his colors were Jack Atkin and Nealon. In the biggest surprise of the 1910 racing season, Jack Atkin won the Dominion Handicap at Fort Erie and its $10,000 winner's purse (about $2.1 million in 2023 terms).

Barney was recognized in 1909 as Missouri's premier turf man and raiser of horses. In 1913, he had seventy-five horses available for the season. By 1919, Barney Schreiber had passed away at the age of fifty-three.

6

HENRY "KID" BECKER

BOOKMAKER

Another kingpin at the beginning of the twentieth century was Henry "Kid" Becker. Louis Cella and the Kid probably passed one another on the streets of St. Louis.

The St. Louis and East Side tracks closed in 1905, but that didn't stop the betting. Becker was a close St. Louis ally of Mont Tennes from Chicago. He helped to begin Mont's wire service. The relatively immediate messaging of race results from tracks that were open provided the mechanism to continue bookmaking without a bookie having to be at the track, as in the past.

Henry Becker was born in South St. Louis in 1882 to a father who was a saloon owner. Henry ran away from home at ten years of age. He returned to care for his widowed mother and two sisters. For a short time in the early 1890s, Henry worked at the *St. Louis Chronicle* newspaper, stacking papers coming off the press. In the early 1900s, he became known as a professional craps shooter and the biggest horse-race handbook man in the city. He operated in the strong belief that all dealings would be honest and lived his life that way. In keeping with the standards of the day, Henry operated from a cigar store at Eighth and Chestnut in downtown St. Louis. He also operated on the East Side.

In addition to closing racetracks, anti-gambling groups were in full force against East Side gambling. The city grand jury issued twenty-six indictments for gambling in East St. Louis in 1907. The charges were for

HENRY "KID" BECKER.

Henry "Kid" Becker, the king of St. Louis handbooks, was the first in St. Louis to use a race wire service. He operated for twenty years in the East Side and in St. Louis. He was only thirty-six at the time of his death in 1919. *St. Louis Post-Dispatch, April 16, 1919.*

dice games and handbooks for betting on horse races. Bookies were operating within places of business, mainly saloons, and many were from St. Louis operating on the East Side. Kid Becker would have been among those indicted. Henry was living at the Royal Hotel at Collinsville and Missouri Avenues in downtown East St. Louis. His indictment was for running a handbook from the saloon of J.T. Inslow at 303 Missouri Avenue, down the street from Becker's hotel.

In 1911, detectives arrested the Kid in St. Louis for operating a handbook and found a check to him signed by Barney Schreiber. He admitted to running a handbook but said he worked on the East Side.

By 1913, Charles Webb, the state attorney of St. Clair County, of which East St. Louis is a part, was identified as being the slayer of gambling. Kid Becker was involved in one raid for running a handbook. Money was taken by Webb's group during the raid. The Kid wanted his money back and sued Webb to recover the $2,000 taken ($389,000 in today's terms).

Becker operated on the basis that he would take a bet on anything and take any side on a wager. He was known as a craps shooter emeritus and king of St. Louis handbook operations. It was said that he operated a vast, well-equipped and organized operation. He encountered no serious police interference. Toward the end for his life, he maintained offices with bookkeepers, stenographers, adding machines, cost accountants, filing cabinets and indexes. His operation spanned both St. Louis and the East Side.

He was accused of making gambling a science. His organization was vast and virtually controlled gambling in St. Louis. He had agents at most street corners, poolrooms and saloons. Someone just needed to say they wanted to bet, and the Becker agent was there to make it.

The Kid had a long winning streak, but it came to an end in 1919, when he was only thirty-six. A robber shot and killed him while he was entering his house. The killer was found, tried and sentenced to life imprisonment. Henry Becker was divorced and had no children. He left his mother an estate of $200,000 ($21 million today). That is the official total. There were rumors that Becker had been doing about $1 million in business a year.

JOHN WALTERS

BETTING COMMISSIONER

John Walters, a Brooklyn native, was a double kingpin in New York. He was essentially the bookmaker to New York society, as well as treasurer of the Robinson Amusement Company, owner of the New Brighton Theater and Casino on Ocean Parkway at Coney Island.

In 1898, at Saratoga Springs, he became clubhouse betting commissioner and would go on to accumulate thirty-five years of betting experience. He was never called before the Jockey Club to explain any of his tactics or transactions.

Walters was born in Brooklyn and began his career by selling programs at racetracks. There was another person around the same time who set the pattern for the type of betting Walters pursued. Frank Warner, from St. Louis, also began selling racetrack programs, at Fairgrounds Track in St. Louis in the late 1880s and early 1890s. At this time, bookmakers worked at designated places at the tracks. People sitting in the grandstand had to approach the bookmaker of choice to place their bet. One day, Frank was approached by a lady in the grandstand and asked if he would place a bet for her. He did; she won and rewarded him. Warner now had a new job. He eventually employed more than one hundred boys to place bets for the female occupants in the grandstand. By 1894, he had taken the same thing to Chicago's Washington Park racetrack and then tried to do the same at Saratoga Springs in New York. The management wasn't interested, but the track owners saw the benefit. Frank installed a troop of betting commissioners in the stands and had them corral a heavy play for his

John Walters.

John Walters of Brooklyn was known as a clubhouse commissioner with a large following at Saratoga. He was especially known as the betting commissioner for high-society members from 1905 until his 1929 death in Paris. Brooklyn Daily Eagle, *August 19, 1928.*

own book. After that, the clubhouse commissioner job position was established and made its appearance in the East. John Walters rose to take that position. Warner switched careers and went on to serve for twenty years representing St. Louis in the Missouri State Senate.

Johnny Walters came to fame in racing circles when he oversaw all racing interests of William C. Whitney, secretary of the navy under President Grover Cleveland, and continued with his son and other family members.

He was considered a high-class betting commissioner, taking big wagers and, likewise, big chances at times. He started with the Whitney family; other members of the clubhouse regulars also became his customers. He was known to have a large following from society's "Four Hundred." (Ward McAllister reportedly coined the term *the Four Hundred*, declaring that there were "only 400 people in fashionable New York Society." According to him, this was the number of people in New York who really mattered, those who felt at ease in the ballrooms of high society.) In addition to handling their money and overseeing the higher level of bets, Walters also placed his own bets.

Public information is limited, but he handicapped and placed bets for his own account. One brought him $100,000 on a race ($25 million in today's terms). Some of those funds were probably used with George Robinson. In 1904, Walters and Robinson built the New Brighton Theater at Coney Island, which enjoyed the patronage of the regulars of Brighton Beach, Sheepshead Bay, and Gravesend tracks.

For years, Walters was the kingpin by being the betting clubhouse commissioner at all the leading tracks. An indication of his success as the society betting commissioner was his $35,000 donation to a World War I bond drive. His son was serving as a U.S. Marine during the war. That donation amounts to $3.8 million in today's dollars.

Walters passed away in 1929 while on holiday with his wife and three daughters in Paris. He was fifty-eight years old. The family house in Brooklyn was left to his wife, as was $250,000—a significant sum for a quiet betting whiz and theater follower.

THOMAS "CHICAGO" O'BRIEN

TRACK BETTOR

The largest racetrack bettor at this time was considered to be Thomas O'Brien. He was born in 1867 to Irish immigrant parents in Chicago. His family moved when he was a youngster to Kansas and Iowa and then back to Chicago. In between these moves, Thomas's mother passed away. His father remarried and had two additional children.

Thomas became a bricklayer when he returned to Chicago. Around 1902, on a rainy day, he went to the Hawthorne Racetrack. Thomas made bets on the favorite in six races, all to place third, and he won them all. He continued using that system and went to Big Jim O'Leary's poolroom for bookmakers to play full time.

A professional gambler noticed Thomas and suggested he go east. He followed that advice and continued his fascination with horse racing and betting. In 1903, Thomas married Ernestine Schwartz in Chicago. In 1904, his daughter Virginia was born.

By 1905, Thomas O'Brien and his family had set up their residence in Brooklyn. A second daughter arrived in 1908. The family stayed in New York City, living in Brooklyn and Manhattan. The daughters were raised in New York City and were married there. O'Brien made quite an impact at New York State racetracks, where he was given the nickname "Chicago," as he had been living in that city. Other New York–area tracks also felt his presence.

In 1905, the family was highlighted by the *Buffalo Times*, which made note of Thomas's horse-race betting success. O'Brien was called the newest and

Thomas O'Brien and his family are shown in a 1905 photo, highlighting his betting approach. O'Brien went from being a bricklayer to a millionaire and became the most noted racetrack player in the country. Buffalo Times, *September 24, 1905.*

nerviest "Turf Plunger," an old term for a horse-race bettor winning the money. O'Brien's significance lay in his new approach to betting. Winning required careful study and knowledge of Thoroughbreds and track conditions.

In a nutshell, he bet on the favorites to place third, not to win. His tactic paid off a considerable number of times. Thomas studied the horses and never solicited inside information from owners or trainers. He never talked to the jockeys, unless they were his own riders. He began this way and eventually built up a stable of horses of his own. He made sure to enter his horses in the New York races, with Saratoga being a prime one. He did most of his betting on horses he didn't own. In any case, they were very big bets for the time.

O'Brien focused on tracks at Fort Erie in Canada; in New York State at Saratoga Springs and New York City; in Baltimore, Maryland; in New Orleans; and, of course, in Kentucky. With its closure of tracks, Chicago did not become part of his agenda.

O'Brien passed away at Saratoga Springs in 1931 at the age of sixty-six. The man with the nickname "Chicago" who spent the better part of his later life in New York was brought back to Chicago for burial. At the time of his death, O'Brien was thought to have bet more money than any other person. After his death, tracks in Maryland lamented his passing by noticing the decline in pari-mutuel betting. The average handle was $350,000 ($44 million today). "Chicago" was known to have bet around $20,000 a day at the tracks—a pretty good portion for one person. Tim Mara, a high-stakes bookmaker and bettor at the same time, related that he would see O'Brien bet at least this much every day.

9

SENORITA CONCEPCION DE HARA

FARO GAMBLER

One pastime hugely popular in the Wild West mining towns was a card game called faro. It virtually disappeared by about 1915. The better pace and costs of roulette and blackjack to players and casino owners spelled the end of faro.

In 1900, faro made its way to New York, Chicago, Philadelphia and St. Louis. The confiscation of faro paraphernalia was well documented by police in these cities. According to the *Chicago Tribune* in 1903, faro was considered a major game in the city. Mont Tennes is shown opening a new casino on Chicago's North Side at 14 Federal Street in 1910, after his previous one at 125 Clark was demolished by a bombing. Faro was considered a major draw. The *New York Sun* reported faro deal boxes and equipment being confiscated at a significant cost from Honest John Kelly's gambling house on Manhattan's West Forty-Fourth Street in 1913.

Professional gamblers persisted over time, from the riverboat days to the mining towns. One professional gambler made quite a name with the game of faro. In the mining towns of Arizona, New Mexico, California and Texas, faro was in its prime, and this player attained the status of a kingpin. In 1903, Senorita Concepcion de Hara was twenty-two years old and had been playing as a professional gambler for two years. She was at the time one of the few women in the world who made gambling a profession. Originally from Guanajuato, Mexico, de Hara moved with her family as a young girl to Juarez, across from El Paso, Texas.

Left: Senorita Concepion de Hara, a professional gambler, is seen in a drawing. Chicago Tribune, *October 25, 1903.*

Right: A drawing of de Hara at a faro game. She made a fortune playing this game. Chicago Tribune, *October 25, 1903.*

She learned English and was taught faro by her father, who studied the mathematics of the game to achieve success. She became a faro dealer in El Paso at age twenty. In 1901, she made $80 in one week of dealing faro, the equivalent of $3,000 today. With her brother Manuel as a companion, de Hara went on the road to try her luck. She traveled from town to town with Manuel and, most of the time, won big. She banked a fortune but was sure to send her winnings to her father after leaving each town.

All the gamblers held de Hara in high esteem. They were not happy about losing but were accepting of her skills. When word spread that she had arrived in a new town, gamblers journeyed from miles around to see her in action.

All her games were honest and straightforward. The Wild West attitude prevailed: Pay attention to the cards and winning, not what the person you're playing against looks like. Such success was quite an achievement for anybody, let alone a young lady from Mexico.

10

HONEST JOHN KELLY

CASINO OWNER

In the same era, there was Honest John Kelley. He was the kingpin of gambling houses in New York City in the 1900s.

Gambling was illegal but still very common in New York at the turn of the twentieth century. Games of chance such as cards, dice and numbers, as well as sports betting, particularly for horse racing, were popular pastimes. Gambling took place in New York's upper-class private clubs.

Honest John was a gambler. He wagered large sums with the bookies in Manhattan and at tracks across the country. He also focused on casino and table games. Kelly ran one of the most popular gambling houses.

In 1905, Kelly appeared before a justice and testified that he had been nine years in the gambling business and occupied the houses at 137, 139 and 141 West Forty-First Street. His business was raided, and a large quantity of valuable gambling paraphernalia was taken and slated to be destroyed. He was given immunity, but a search warrant was still issued.

In 1912, it was reported that the gambling houses—mainly in Manhattan, but also in Brooklyn—paid for protection. A price list was worked out. Big gamblers like Honest John were assessed around $500 a month (in the $30,000 range in 2023 terms); smaller gamblers were assessed in the range of $50 to $300 per month.

By 1913, Honest John was operating at 136 West Forty-Fourth Street. His place was raided along with William Husteed's next door and Maxey Blumenthal's at 161 across the street. At 165 West Forty-Seventh Street, Popper & Delacys was operating, and Arnold Rothstein was operating at

108 West Forty-Sixth. Lou Ludium was at 168 West Forty-Eighth, and Bob Smith worked out of 128 West Forty-Eighth. This was like a who's who of the best and biggest gamblers of the day. They were all visited by the police. Gaming equipment, including faro layouts and deal boxes, poker tables, roulette wheels and cards, was taken to the police station. Dice tables and bushels of chips were confiscated. The value of all paraphernalia taken was estimated at between $6,000 and $10,000 ($350,000 to $600,000 in 2023). No one was arrested. We can guess that Kelly's monthly payments helped that along.

Honest John Kelly

John Kelly, shown shortly before his death, operated one of the most popular gambling houses in New York City from the 1890s. New York Daily News, *November 16, 1925.*

The story goes that Honest John taught Arnold Rothstein how to gamble. Somehow, that honesty escaped Arnold, as he is the person accused in the infamous Black Sox World Series scandal of 1919.

Honest John didn't focus only on table games. It was reported that, on a visit to Chicago's racetracks early in the 1903 season, Kelly admitted to losing $20,000 on one bet (around $1.2 million in 2023). This was in addition to the $125,000 in bets over the duration of his visit.

Honest John earned his name. In 1905, during a period of anti-gambling, the police kept telling the district attorney there was not a single gambler in town they could find to serve with a subpoena. Kelly voluntarily went to the DA's office and told him of the gambling houses he was openly operating at 141 and 127 West Forty-First Street. He said he never paid any money for protection but that he had friends higher up in the police department who saw to it that he was not disturbed. At the time Kelly was doing this, the prosecutor sent police to the spots and removed gambling devices.

John was married twice and had a daughter by his first wife. He lived a long life for his time, passing away at seventy in 1925.

11

MONT TENNES

CASINO, BOOKIE, WIRE SERVICE

n Chicago, Mont Tennes became a multiple kingpin. He operated bookmaking on the city's North Side, then created the first wire service devoted to horse-race results that could be sent to other bookies across the United States. The question surrounding Mont Tennes was how he parlayed a Chicago handbook into a multimillion-dollar business and became the brains behind a nationwide race-reporting wire service.

Mont Tennes was born in Chicago in 1873 and started working as a messenger boy; even then, he was handy with the dice. He started taking bets on horses in the 1890s. He then opened a handbook and added others until he had a dozen by 1910. At the same time, Mont operated gambling houses. There was trouble galore for Mont and other gamblers between 1907 and 1909. There were multiple bombings, and Mont was a victim of five dynamite blasts at his various locations. His operation at 135 Center Avenue was blown up. A blast wrecked his home at 404 Belden Avenue and another of his store at 125 Clark. At the time, it was reported that Mont and Big Jim O'Leary were the heads of an organized syndicate, Mont on the North Side and Big Jim on the South. Pat O'Malley, a First Ward politician, was also rumored to be a part of the syndicate. The anti-gambling crowd believed that as long as there was gambling, there would be bombing. There were thirty-one bombings between 1907 and 1909.

Mont bought several saloons in this period and had several handbooks in operation. By 1910, he had opened a new gambling house at 14 Federal Street that featured craps tables and a faro table. Luxury handbooks didn't come into existence until after 1920. In 1910, Mont's places were generally dingy. Only the results of a race could be heard, and no one was ever sure they were right. Mont figured the handbook needed fast and accurate information directly from the track. Gradually, he got the idea of setting up a service and selling it. Around 1905, he established the General News Bureau. Eventually, it became one of the country's least-known but biggest monopolies and made tremendous profits. Evidently, a truce was made between gamblers and the anti- crowd by 1910, and Mont and his fellow gamblers operated without the continuing bombings. It is believed that by 1910 there were five hundred gambling venues in the city and that the gamblers' collective daily income was $500,000 ($107 million today). It didn't hurt that Mont was reported to have contributed to the mayoral election at the time in the amount of $20,000. Protection payments were probably also part of the truce.

Mont Tennes created a national horse-race betting wire service in the early 1900s. He left a 1941 estate valued at $400 million in 2023 terms. *Ancestry. com, Tennes public family tree, circa 1940.*

One thing Mont didn't participate in was the fix of the 1919 World Series. Supposedly, about two months before the Series began, he warned of an effort to fix it. Mont declined to participate because he couldn't believe that the game could be dishonest. He subsequently lost $30,000 on the White Sox

His start in the information service wasn't pretty. He would buy a building overlooking a racetrack and equip it with a lookout and telegraph key linked to his handbooks. It took two people to begin the system: a person at the track watching the race, and a person at the telegraph key sending the information to the handbooks within ten minutes of the end of the race. Mont had a service to sell, and he first went to someone in Cincinnati doing the same thing, getting news from the Kentucky tracks. In arrangements with the Cincinnati person, Mont set up some wires via Indianapolis.

The system worked, and Mont then tied in Kid Becker in St. Louis. Mont then connected with Cincinnati directly. He followed that with linking up with three people in New York City who were gathering race news and using it in New Jersey. In this way, Mont extended his wire east of Cincinnati. Later, he extended to the West Coast, Detroit and New Orleans.

Mont's competition was the regular telegraph service, but it couldn't match what he was giving bettors. He got the entries, track conditions, odds, scratches and results accurately and quickly. He covered all the tracks, wherever horses were being raced in the United States, Canada, Mexico and Cuba.

Sometime after General News Bureau was flourishing, Mont took in Jack Lynch as a partner. Jack was a bookmaker on the city's West Side. He handled some of Mont's handbooks and worked with General News. Speculation was that Jack was brought in as a representative for certain political elements.

When the gangster Al Capone came to Chicago and began to organize the handbooks, Tennes saw it was time to quit. In 1927, he sold his portion of General News Bureau to Mo Annenberg; Jack Lynch maintained his interest. By 1934, Annenberg had bought out Lynch's interests and created the Nationwide News Service, which was dissolved in 1939. It was then reorganized again as Continental Press, with James Ragen of Chicago as one of the partners. By 1946, Continental Press was under the control of the Capone syndicate after Ragen was killed by the Capone group. By 1952, a federal tax law on gamblers had been passed. This effectively closed the service.

Mont passed away in 1941 at age sixty-three. He operated a successful real estate business after selling his interest in General News. He left behind an estate valued at $5 million (over $400 million today). One of the last of his philanthropic gifts was providing a yearly gift of $10,000 toward the upkeep of a "charter home" for boys known as Camp Honor.

12

MOSES "MO" ANNENBERG

PUBLISHER, WIRE SERVICE

To put things into context, Mont created a nationwide wire service that fed into every handbook in the United States. It gave bookies immediate race results at multiple tracks, and this kept bookies in operation and their endeavors running smoothly. This was combined with the *Daily Racing Form*, which provided information for handicapping horses at different tracks daily. Every bookmaker would surely have had a copy of the newspaper and would have furnished other copies to all the bettors who frequented the handbook's physical locations.

Fred Brunnell ran the newspaper, and Mont Tennes operated the wire service. In 1922, Mo Annenberg made an offer to Brunell and bought the newspaper.

Moses was born in 1878 in what was known at the time as East Prussia. By 1885, Moses and his family had immigrated to Chicago. In 1900, Moses, now known as Mo, was twenty-two and recently married. William Randolph Hearst, the biggest publisher of newspapers, was in a circulation battle with the eight newspapers in Chicago. Mo got a job to increase circulation and succeeded. He wanted to achieve success on his own, and he moved his family to Milwaukee to increase circulation of Chicago newspapers there. In 1917, he took control of the *Wisconsin News*, owned by Arthur Brisbane, which was sold to Hearst. He then moved to New York to oversee all of Hearst's newspaper and magazine publications. He wound up doing well and had a plush apartment in Manhattan and a place on Long Island.

Moses "Mo" Annenberg created a national monopoly of horse-race betting through the acquisition of Mont Tennes's wire service and the *Daily Racing Form*. New York Daily News, *July 2, 1940.*

In 1922, Arthur Brisbane let Mo know about Frank Brunell's small publication at the time, *Daily Racing Form*. Mo approached Brunell and brought $400,000 in cash and took over ownership. Mo applied his circulation experience to dominating the race information service. By 1926, this took up more of his time, and he left Hearst.

In 1927, Mo bought a 50 percent share of Mont's wire service and by 1934 had 100 percent control. Mo became not only a betting kingpin but also created a monopoly. In 1936, he purchased the *Philadelphia Inquirer*, which he felt had prestige and class. He worked his circulation magic, and it became a major success.

Unfortunately for Mo, his race information monopoly brought the attention of federal agencies, and they went after him for income tax evasion. Mo lost and went to prison, having to shut down his wire service in 1939. He came out of prison in 1942 and passed away at the Mayo Clinic shortly thereafter.

His family maintained control of the *Daily Racing Form*, which was taken over by his son Walter, who also oversaw the *Philadelphia Inquirer*. Walter operated the publications under the ownership name Triangle Publications. Walter created a series of other highly profitable publications. In 1988, Walter sold *Daily Racing Form* to News America. The publication was sold a few more times, finally resting in 2023 at a private equity LLC.

13

BIG JIM O'LEARY

SOUTH SIDE GAMBLER

Just as the Kid operated at the same time as friendly competitors, Mont Tennes had a betting kingpin operating in Chicago at the same time: Jim O'Leary. While Mont was on the North Side, Big Jim operated on the South Side.

James Patrick O'Leary was born in Chicago in 1870. His parents were Irish immigrants. The Great Chicago Fire was alleged to have begun in a horse barn belonging to the O'Leary family.

As a teenager, Jim worked for local bookies. He eventually became a bookmaker himself in Indiana. He went bankrupt and returned to Chicago to work at the Union Stockyards, where he gained the name "Big Jim." In the early 1890s, he left the stockyards and opened a saloon on Halstead Street. The place included a Turkish bath, a restaurant, a billiards room and a bowling alley. O'Leary posted detailed track results and other betting information near the entrance to the stockyards. He soon began operating a pool hall and book parlor in the rear of the saloon.

He soon became one of the leading gamblers in Chicago and was known for taking bets on a steamship. This venture failed by 1907, as police raided the ship whenever it docked. In the same year, Chicago's crime lord at the time died, and Big Jim took control of gambling on the city's Southwest Side, around the stockyards. Despite numerous raids by police, O'Leary was found guilty of gambling just once in his thirty-nine-year career. The perception was that he and Mont Tennes controlled the city's police. That was probably an accurate perception.

James O'Leary was known as the "Prince of Gamblers" on Chicago's South Side. He was known to bet large amounts on anything until his passing in 1925. Chicago Tribune, *March 9, 1921.*

Jim was not only physically big, but also would be the betting commissioner size. In 1904, it was reported that he organized a pool of $500,000 to go to New York to make a book. Of course, this was with the blessing of Tammany Hall. There is no word on the result, but since he stayed in business for over twenty years after that, it is assumed that he did just fine. He took on large bets, not only for horse racing. In the election year of 1916, he had to pay off $650,000 ($88 million in 2023) on the presidential election; he chose Charles Evans Hughes over Woodrow Wilson. Big Jim would bet on anything from horse races, prizefights and baseball to the weather and presidential elections.

Big Jim, the so-called Prince of Gamblers in his time, passed away in 1925, leaving his wife, two sons and three daughters. He was only fifty-six and died of heart-related causes. He left no will. The family said he had left $10,000. Many at the time raised their eyebrows at the relatively small amount, considering the size of his bets and payouts.

14

BROADWAY JACK DOYLE

HANDICAPPER

Broadway Jack Doyle, in New York City, operated in the same vein as other oddsmakers did in other parts of the United States. Jack became a kingpin, setting odds on the outcome at various betting venues. John T. "Jack" Doyle came to New York in 1899 from Springfield, Massachusetts, working as a racetrack bookmaker and sheet writer.

In those days, a person who did much betting was considered a social pariah. But betting flourished, stimulated by the Irish Sweepstakes, contract bridge, golf, college football and the society aspects of racing.

In 1906, Jack opened a combination billiards parlor, restaurant and bar at Forty-Second and Broadway. He started the business with John McGraw, the New York Giants baseball manager, and Tod Sloan, a famous jockey of the day. Jack wound up as the sole owner after a couple of years and operated it until 1937. Jack was able to draw an opening-night list of notables, including names that might be familiar today: Willie Hoppe, John McGraw, Christy Mathewson, Jim Corbett, Eddie Foy, Kid McCoy, Billy Murray, Weber & Fields, Pat Powers, Ike Thompson, Mike Donlin, Roger Bresnahan and John T. Brush.

Jack became known as New York's unofficial "betting commissioner" and the "Wizard of Odds." His odds, particularly on baseball, were the only ones many conservative newspapers would print. During Jack's time on Broadway, he claimed to have seen America become the greatest gambling country in the world. He was an associate of celebrities, sports figures, show-business people and politicians He insisted that he was not a betting commissioner,

JACK DOYLE

John T. Doyle was a widely known betting commissioner from New York. He set the accepted odds on most sporting events that were used throughout the country. *The State (Charleston, SC), October 2, 1935.*

but rather a price-maker. He claimed to have never taken a commission nor won a quarter on betting, similar to Tom Kearney. Jack essentially became known nationally for setting the odds-on baseball, boxing, football and elections.

He moved from his spot on Forty-Second Street because of a heart ailment and relocated to the Central Park Hotel. He kept up his operations from there and attended most major sports events. In those days, he concentrated on baseball. He did his last betting on the 1942 World Series between the St. Louis Cardinals and New York Yankees.

In a 1942 interview, Jack listed the betting sports in order of importance: horse racing, football, boxing, baseball, basketball and ice hockey. He went on to say that on eight or nine Saturdays during the college football season, there was more wagering on football than during the entire baseball season, including the World Series.

Broadway Jack was prescient in his analysis, considering where sports betting is in 2023. Football is clearly the dominant sport. Horse racing is still going, but it isn't number one anymore. College football is still played on Saturdays, and Sundays are the domain of professional football—both viewing and betting.

Jack passed away from heart issues at sixty-seven years of age in 1942. His betting advice on various sports odds and point spreads resonated with another betting kingpin.

15

TOM KEARNEY

BOOKMAKER, ODDSMAKER

In his time, Kid Becker was involved with another bookmaker operating on the East Side and in St. Louis: Tom Kearney. Tom operated from a cigar store at 407 Walnut in downtown St. Louis and at 100 West Broadway, just across the Eads Bridge in East St. Louis. Tom worked with the Kid in suing to recover $2,000 in funds from Charles Webb's raid in 1913 (see chapter 6).

In 1910, while Tom was operating his East Side handbook, there was a winning parlay from the racetrack in Jacksonville, Florida, that had a nine-to-one shot, along with a five-to-one shot. Bookmakers across the country were out $500,000 ($108 million today). Tom suffered a loss of $30,000. Kid Becker also lost money, about $3,000, which he didn't want to pay. He thought the parlay was a sting setup.

Tom was born on the South Side of St. Louis in 1871 to Irish immigrants who became saloonkeepers. He passed away at the age of sixty-six in 1936 and was eulogized as a bookmaker-philanthropist. He led a colorful and eventful life as a betting kingpin and oddsmaker in the vein of Jack Doyle and Tom Shaw.

He operated what became known as the "Big Store" at Fourth and Walnut in downtown St. Louis, just a block from the Old Cathedral, his parish. The "Cigar Store," which did sell tobacco products, was operated by him from 1900 to 1932. Due to road construction, he moved to a hotel up the street with his wife and opened another store across the street, operating it from 1932 until he passed away in 1936. Kid Becker's

Tom Kearney

Tom Kearney was a betting commissioner in the East Side and in St. Louis from 1900 to 1936. He was highly respected. He handled high-dollar bets and set betting odds throughout the Midwest. St. Louis Post-Dispatch, *April 17, 1932*.

place was a little over four blocks away, and they pretty much operated the handbooks in both St. Louis and the East Side. When the police became too touchy, Tom and Becker would vary their base between Illinois and Missouri. After the Kid's passing, Tom established himself as the betting commissioner, taking on all the big bets throughout the country. He set the odds for horse racing and other activities and was quoted for them throughout the country, but his major influence was in the Midwest.

The image on the following page shows his odds in January for the 1934 baseball season for each team. This was published in the *St. Louis Post-Dispatch* for all bettors to contemplate.

As talked about earlier, he made good on a questionable parlay bet in 1910, and he did the same thing in 1924, paying out $74,000. Kearney, along with Tom Shaw in New York, were the only bookmakers in the country who were able to pay off a Kentucky Derby win that broke the rest of the bookmakers, who couldn't pay off. The two Toms were renowned for this effort for the rest of their bookmaking days. They made big bets, set odds and paid off, Shaw on the East Coast and Kearney in the Midwest. Their forecasts of horse-racing winners and results in other sports were published in newspapers and followed by the bettors.

As a child, Kearney sold newspapers on the street corner. He then worked for a while at the Vulcan Iron Works and wound up as a bartender at a popular downtown St. Louis saloon. While there, he cut in as a bookmaker on the horse races being run in the St. Louis area and in other cities. He made his first venture as a layer of odds and would cover everything from a dime up to his bankroll. He continued with this and opened operations at a couple of places until the reform movement hit in 1904. Just like Louis Cella, he took off for Hot Springs, Arkansas. Contrary to Louis's purchase of the racetrack in Hot Springs, Tom operated a large and noted gambling house. With reform toned down, he came back and opened the Big Store on Walnut and the East Side operation on Broadway. Besides his work on horse races, Tom became one of the biggest layer of odds on elections, baseball games and prize fights, making a fortune off them.

Tom and his wife had no children. He became noted for his Christmastime gestures. He sent money, food, cigars and cigarettes to inmates of penitentiaries, especially those from St. Louis. He felt that society was to blame for many men finding themselves behind bars, and he wanted to help. He also made sure that everyone at City Hospital had turkey at Christmas. In another gesture, he bought up a series of cemetery plots so that acquaintances who couldn't afford one would have a final resting place.

In St. Louis, Tom Kearney was the "Ace of the Midwest" in odds making; Tom claimed to never have bet himself. He was the betting commissioner for not only St. Louis and the East Side but also for a good portion of the country.

Voices of Spring.

THE birds aren't chirping, yet, but Tom Kearney is. Probably influenced by the fact that the ground hogs have been gamboling around, looking at their shadows long before the appointed day, the veteran today liberated his hardy annual odds on the major league baseball races—a sure harbinger of returning spring, at least in the hearts of the fans.

Although the vernal equinox is nearly two months distant and the opening of the baseball season three weeks later than that, Kearney announces the following deductions with regard to the probable finish of the two flag marathons, the chances of the respective clubs being reflected in these odds:

NATIONAL.		AMERICAN.	
Giants	2-1	Senators	3-2
Cubs	3-1	Yankees	5-2
Pirates	3-1	White Sox	8-1
Cardinals	6-1	Tigers	8-1
Braves	10-1	Red Sox	10-1
Dodgers	15-1	Indians	10-1
Phillies	30-1	Athletics	10-1
Reds	100-1	Browns	100-1

Tom Kearney's odds-on preseason picks of the baseball teams for the upcoming 1934 season. St. Louis Post-Dispatch, *January 24, 1934.*

The odds from both Toms were followed intently in the newspapers. The accompanying image provides a listing of their odds, showing the difference in their levels. The rationale for the difference is that Kearney's is based on much of the Midwest, and Shaw's reflects the majority of the East Coast.

When Tom Kearney passed away, his close competitor, James J. Carroll, took over. They were both born in St. Louis of Irish immigrant parents and established operations in both St. Louis and the East Side. Both their parents were saloonkeepers, Tom's on the South Side and Jimmy's on the North Side.

16

TOM SHAW

BOOKMAKER, ODDSMAKER

Tom Shaw was a protégé of Barney Schreiber. Big Tom Shaw became a kingpin and relished being known as the "betting commissioner." He was big in betting and big in physical size, standing a trim six feet, three inches tall and weighing 220 pounds.

In New York, Shaw ruled the roost on horse racing. He was known in New York and influenced the level of betting throughout the United States. Betting on political elections was a popular gambling activity. Between 1868 and 1940, there was a considerable scale of betting on U.S. presidential elections. This betting was centered in New York, which accounted for over half of the activity. The amount of money spent on election betting was occasionally surpassed by the amount of money traded on Wall Street's stock markets.

Tom was born in 1879 in New Orleans. His father, an Irish immigrant, was a confectioner who owned trotters. His mother was born in Louisiana. Tom first won prominence as an amateur bike rider but never turned professional. One of his chief biking rivals was Charles Howard. In 1905, Howard opened a bike repair shop in San Francisco. He made millions in automobiles and owned horses. He went from bikes to horse racing and became owner of the infamous racehorse Seabiscuit.

Tom went from bikes to gaming as a clerk in the gambling room of Parson and Davies at Canal and St. Charles Streets in New Orleans. From there, he teamed up with Barney Schreiber, the man from St. Louis who owned the horse Jack Atkin. Barney and Tom then moved west, where they controlled the books at the old Santa Anita track in Arcadia, near Los Angeles. Then they moved to New Orleans, where Barney's horse proved the oddsmakers wrong. With the winner's purse and bookies' money, Barney, Tom and Jack Atkin made their way to New York's tracks.

Shaw brought with him a profound knowledge of western horses and chucking it in on them. In 1908, Tom won races with Nealon and Jack Atkin to the tune of about $50,000 each a few different times (about $11 million in 2023).

Tom was part of Barney's Jack Atkin horse ownership, winning the Dominion Handicap purse of $10,000 ($2.1 million in 2023). Barney and Tom cleaned out the books that predicted their horse would lose; they gained about $100,000.

Tom went on to set up his own bookmaking operation. He operated from New York as an oddsmaker and bookmaker and earned East Coast and national prominence. Joining him was Philip Kim, who served as cashier for over thirty years with Tom. Philip was born in St. Louis and worked with Barney Schreiber before teaming up with Tom. Philip's son Philip Jr. also worked with Tom before and after his father's passing.

Above: Tom Shaw invested more than forty years of active business to become the dean of New York bookmakers. He was a highly respected odds setter in the East. New York Daily News, *June 12, 1935.*

Opposite: Tom Kearney and Tom Shaw became nationally known for their posting of odds. A side-by-side comparison is shown for the 1933 Kentucky Derby. St. Louis Post-Dispatch, *February 26, 1933.*

Tom became known as the "betting commissioner" in New York. There were betting commissioners in other cities, including Chicago and St. Louis. Essentially, these people took on large-dollar bets. In most cases, they tried to "lay off" the big bets, which meant having other bookies take a portion of the bet so that no one was overextended should the bet have to be paid off.

Tom took pride in never refusing to take a large bet, either keeping it all or trying to lay it off. Even more important was his integrity. In 1924, all the future book bets on the Kentucky Derby proved wrong. This meant that all of the bookies who took in the bets had to pay them out. There

The bookmakers rate Cavalcade, Mata Hari, Sir Thomas, Bazaar and Discovery as the "big five" of the derby contenders. Odds on the fourteen leading nominees, laid by Tom Shaw of New York and Tom Kearney of St. Louis, future book operators, follow:

Horse	Shaw	Kearney
Cavalcade	3-1	4-1
Mata Hari	5-1	4-1
Sir Thomas	6-1	6-1
Bazaar	8-1	10-1
Discovery	10-1	8-1
Singing Wood	20-1	8-1
Sgt. Byrne	15-1	10-1
Riskulus	15-1	10-1
Agrarian	12-1	20-1
Time Supply	30-1	20-1
Peace Chance	30-1	20-1
Speedmore	30-1	40-1
Spy Hill	30-1	40-1
Blue Again	30-1	40-1

The betting commissioners post their odds according to how much money is wagered with them on each horse. Some of the discrepancies in the list are accounted for by the fact that Shaw handles eastern money largely, while Kearney receives the investments of westerners. Cavalcade and Discovery are eastern nominees, while Mata Hari, Sir Thomas and Bazaar are western hopefuls.

were only two bookies in the country who did: Tom Shaw and Tom Kearney of St. Louis. Kearney had to pay out $74,000. The betting community took note of bets and had to pay them out. There were only two bookies in the country who did pay them out. Both men were universally recognized as betting commissioners on a national level, Shaw on the East Coast and Kearney in the Midwest.

The accompanying image is a 1934 article from the *Democrat and Chronicle* newspaper of Rochester, New York, showing the odds quoted in April for the upcoming Kentucky Derby. Both Kearney and Shaw provided their listings for all to contemplate when deciding a bet.

In addition to laying the horses, Tom Shaw also played them. He bet on the ponies as well as quoted odds against them. He truly beat the odds of his day by living to be ninety-nine years old, passing away in 1978.

17

TIM MARA

BOOKMAKER, SPORTS TEAM OWNER

Tim Mara was born in 1887 of Irish immigrant parents on the Lower East Side of Manhattan. His dad was a police officer who died before Tim was born, leaving his mother a widow with Tim and his older brother, John.

Tim's mathematics education ended in grade school. He did, however, acquire enough of it to be successful in the fastest game around, bookmaking horses. And he did so on a robust scale.

He started as a child being paid to watch out for ticket speculators in front of the New Amsterdam Theater. His brother did some work with the Ziegfeld Theater, running errands and placing bets. Tim was a big man, standing six feet tall and weighing two hundred pounds. He was hearty, always laughing and very sentimental. He was a member of Tammany Hall and a friend to politicians James Farley and Al Smith. In other words, he had significant political connections.

It was reported that for recreation he went to the movies or astonished his friends by solving intricate arithmetical problems without pencil and paper. Tim shared Tom Kearney's generous character. At Christmas, he sent baskets of food containing dressed chicken with all the trimmings. He did this for years and had to stop when the number of baskets reached the thousands.

In his younger days, Tim's interests and connections were in the horse-racing and boxing worlds. He was especially known for arranging a boxing match of the ages between Jack Dempsey and Gene Tunney. This was a

Bookmaker Tim Mara is seen in 1932 at Saratoga Springs Racetrack. He purchased a money-losing football team in the 1920s. The franchise eventually became the Super Bowl–winning New York Giants. The family is still involved with the team. New York Daily News, *March 22, 1932.*

closely followed match in the United States, and it drew worldwide attention and interest, especially for its era.

Bookmaking at horse races was his biggest interest. At a 1922 Belmont Track race, Tim admitted to dropping $60,000 on a race (about $7 million today). On another occasion, around 1927, he admitted to winning a race event at Saratoga to the tune of $50,000. At one time, Tim quit bookmaking and became involved in the stock brokerage business. He was nearly wiped out. He also took a chance at importing Scotch whisky after Prohibition, but that didn't work out.

In 1934, when open betting returned to New York racetracks, Tim the bookmaker could be found at Saratoga. On weekdays, he handled between $10,000 and $15,000; on Saturdays and holidays, $30,000 and up.

One thing did work out and continues to operate to this day. In 1925, Tim wound up paying $2,500 for a professional football franchise, the New York Giants. Those were lean times for professional football, and Tim suffered a $50,000 loss in his first year in the business. Bookmaking and betting wins helped support his venture. Things continued for a while along this path. But Tim's oft-quoted line was, "Thar's gold in them thar hills." How true that turned out to be. Tim and his brother, John, began operating the franchise as their main business. Pro football started to establish a firmer foothold in society. In later years, Tim's children, John and Wellington, and their children, took overactive management of the team. The Mara family still operates the franchise, although with 50 percent interest, since one of the Mara brothers sold their share. The franchise is considered to have a 2023 value in the range of $6 billion. Tim really did find gold in those New York hills.

18

CHARLES BIDWILL SR.

TRACK OWNER, SPORTS TEAM OWNER

In the 1920s, Charles Bidwill entered the racetrack scene in Chicago. He was quoted as saying that racing is the greatest sport in the world.

The Corrigan family opened Chicago's Hawthorne Racecourse in 1891 and closed it in 1905, when Illinois followed Missouri in its closure of racetracks. The family sold it to Thomas Carey in 1909. He tried a short meet in 1916 but then closed down until reopening legally in 1922. Charley Bidwill took an ownership interest in Hawthorne at that time. The track has remained in operation in various forms up to today. The Carey family continues to maintain their ownership interest.

Bidwill was born in Chicago in 1895. He went to Loyola University Law School and fought in World War I. He worked as an assistant corporation counsel under Chicago mayor Big Bill Thompson. After a while, he became head of Bentley-Murray Company, a firm that printed racetrack programs, admissions and mutuel tickets as well as tickets for other sporting events.

For a time, he was also head of the Chicago Stadium Operating Company, working to bring prizefights and six-day bicycle races to the city.

By 1928, Bidwill had put his love for racing into action. He purchased racehorses and began to run them at different tracks. In the same year, he became secretary of the Illinois Turf Association, with plans to invest at least $50,000 (close to $4.8 million today) in the racing game in an effort to bolster his stable. In 1927, Al Capone opened up Sportsman's Park Racetrack adjacent to Hawthorne.

Charles Bidwill Sr. of Chicago owned several betting ventures. He purchased the money-losing Chicago Cardinals football team in the 1930s. That team, which remains in the family, moved, and became the St. Louis Cardinals before moving again and becoming the Arizona Cardinals. *Collyer's Eye, December 8, 1928.*

Capone's racecourse was for dogs, and betting was generally fixed by Capone. Of course, dog racing was illegal. After Capone was taken out of the picture, the track fell into disrepair. By 1937, Charles was being called the "big shot," or, as we are calling him, the "Kingpin of Hawthorne." By 1946, Bidwill was able to purchase Sportsman's Park, and it was fitted for Thoroughbred racing, operating alongside Hawthorne Track. Charles's family maintained its operation after he passed away in 1947. His family held ownership, which was passed to his sons and then grandson. This also applied to Charles's ownership of a women's professional softball team. When still alive, Charles had ceased being part-owner of the American Giants baseball team of the Negro League. He owned four dog tracks at Miami Beach Kennel in Florida for decades. His grandson Charles Bidwill III oversaw the final days of the track and invested $60 million to attempt a combination horse-race track and motor speedway. That did not succeed with the public.

The town of Cicero bought Sportsman's Park for $18 million in 2003. The National Jockey Club, the entity that owned the track, merged with Hawthorne, which now holds Chicago's spring Thoroughbred meet. After its demolition, the former site of Sportsman's Park comprised a Walmart store and a beverage distribution business, and the remainder became parkland. Hawthorne continues to operate as a horse-race track.

During his time in horse racing, Charles took on another sport. In 1933, he was director of the Illinois Turf Association and secretary of the Chicago Businessmen's Racing Association (Hawthorne). He was friends with George Halas, who owned the Chicago Bears professional football team. Halas was facing financial difficulties. Charles invested $5,000 with Halas and the team.

In the same period, Charles was approached by Chicago dentist David Jones, who owned the other pro football team in town, the Cardinals. He wanted to sell the franchise. Charles paid Jones $50,000 ($3 million today). Charles had to divest of his venture with the Bears before buying the

Hawthorne Race Course in Chicago is seen in 2022. It was a major part of the Bidwill family's holdings. The racetrack is still in operation. *Hawthorne Race Course. hawthorneracecourse.com.*

Cardinals. Charles Bidwill passed away in 1947, but the team remains in the family today.

Professional football at the time was nowhere near the level of popularity and financial success it enjoys today. It was reported that the Cardinals cost Charles around $500,000 in losses during his ownership (about $30 million today). He had two sons, Charles II and William. The brothers eventually inherited all of Charley and their mother's estate, worth $10 million. The brothers managed the football team together from around 1962 until 1972. Then the brothers split, with Bill buying Charles II's 50 percent interest and taking over sole management. Charles stayed in Chicago to primarily operate Sportsman's Park's racetrack until his passing. Charles II then took over. The Cardinals moved to St. Louis in 1960, then, under Bill's management, moved to Phoenix in 1986. After Bill's passing, his son, Charles's grandson Michael Bidwill, took charge of the operation.

Charles Bidwill III and his family stayed involved in gambling and came back to St. Louis. Charles III held major ownership with a group of investors that began a casino in 1993. That share was eventually sold in 2012 for $170 million. The casino remains in operation.

19

BETTING ON THE EAST SIDE

1930s-1950

Today's operators are a far cry from the old-time gamblers, but gaming remains. The independent operator has been replaced by a board, shareholders and a multinational scope of operation.

In the 1930s and 1940s, the city of East St. Louis, Illinois, played an outsized role in the open gambling of the time. The city's location and its gaming activities became a major draw, bringing customers and money to the East Side. This drawing power extended throughout southwestern Illinois. Most of the best customers, however, came from its western neighbors in St. Louis.

Gambling at this time was a flourishing and major economic and political force. It was illegal for the most part, but the public still participated.

Contrary to the crackdowns in St. Louis and other parts of the country, the East Side presented a completely different picture. It took a combination of local political acceptance, police cooperation and the strong will of a series of independently owned operators.

The St. Louis side of the river saw a classic approach/avoidance aspect when it came to gambling. The politicians were more reluctant to keep the gamblers in operation and enforced strong shutdowns on occasions. The East Side welcomed the displaced gamblers. Some gamblers set up operations on both sides of the river. Not surprisingly, that continues in 2024. Missouri does not authorize sports betting, while Illinois welcomes it with open arms.

East St. Louis History

East St. Louis, Illinois, was founded in 1797 as Illinoistown and was renamed East St. Louis in 1861, during the Civil War. Illinoistown had a bad reputation due to illicit activities that went on there, hence the change in name.

East St. Louis, across the Mississippi River from St. Louis, could provide more business to the railroads that were built on the East Side. It provided access to the West via the Eads Bridge. Meatpacking became a booming business due to the surrounding Illinois farms and easy transportation across the country. Ease of access and coal and steel production increased facilities and industry in the area.

East St. Louis eventually grew to be the fourth-largest city in Illinois, with a population of 82,000 and a reputation for being where one could always find work. Across the Mississippi, at one time, St. Louis was the fourth-largest city in the United States, with a population of 850,000. Its initial appeal was that it sits on higher ground. The fact that it could provide river access to the railroads was an afterthought.

For close to fifty years, sports betting, casinos and slot machines existed in all forms throughout East St. Louis and nearby communities. A common refrain by St. Louis residents going to gambling and entertainment outlets in Illinois was that they were "going to the East Side."

These places weren't underground but operated in all their glory in relatively open conditions. There were casinos with all the major games, as well as bookmaking and slot machines, all in one place. Gambling facilities were also scattered throughout surrounding communities in several public places.

Collinsville Avenue and Broadway in East St. Louis are seen on a circa 1900s postcard. *Institute for Urban Research.*

Shown here is Eads Bridge, on the St. Louis riverfront, looking toward the East Side. *Study.com*.

The primary gambling and handbook operations were concentrated on Missouri Avenue in downtown East St. Louis, all in proximity to City Hall and police headquarters and across the Eads Bridge from downtown St. Louis.

These were all independently owned and operated establishments. Similar but smaller activities could be found in Belleville, the St. Clair County seat adjacent to East St. Louis, and in neighboring Madison County in Venice and Madison. The East Side's gambling operations helped lay the groundwork for nationwide betting as we know it today. Casinos with all types of table games, slot machines and bookmaking flourished in the open. All were operated by independent owners.

Multiple casinos and handbooks operated in East St. Louis and in neighboring communities. A unique combination of financial acumen and political blindness made it possible for one casino, the Ringside, to become the largest gambling venue in the Midwest at this time.

East Side Kingpins

Three independent owners rose to become kingpins. Adam Fritz, Roy Bowman and Vic Doyle operated close to one another on Missouri and Broadway Avenues in downtown East St. Louis.

Adam "Mulepole" Fritz

Based on reports by the *St. Louis Post-Dispatch*, in 1916, gambling in East St. Louis was being conducted in the open again. It was reported that two large gambling operations were open. One was at Louis Menges's saloon at 100 St. Clair Avenue, which catered to the stockyard workers. The other was at the quarters of the Cahokia Athletic Association at 325 A Missouri Avenue, located close to City Hall and police headquarters. Adam Fritz's nickname, "Mulepole," came from his days shoeing horses and mules at the National City Stockyards. Mulepole operated the association. Both operations had craps games, and Menges also allowed bets on local horse races. In other words, he was operating a handbook.

Mulepole became the kingpin of East Side bookmaking and expanded into St. Louis at the same time. Adam Fritz was born in February 1877 in Toledo, Ohio, and came to East St. Louis as a young man. He went to work as a blacksmith at the National City Stockyards and hit it big one night. He was playing dice in 1912 with his weekly salary of forty-five dollars. He won an interest in the craps table when the house could not pay him off in cash. Later, he began operating tables on his own and then expanded his business to include handbooks.

There are no known public photos of Adam Fritz, but his World War I draft registration provides a clue as to how he looked. Mulepole is listed as having brown hair and brown eyes, standing five feet, seven inches tall and weighing 235 pounds. Calling him burly would be a generous description for the day.

Adam married Mary E. Brewer in 1917; they had no children. In 1936, it was estimated that he had operated twenty-eight handbooks in both St. Louis and Illinois. His worth was estimated at $250,000 at that time (roughly $29 million today). Mulepole dealt with large sums of money from 1912 into the 1940s. In 1927, one of his casinos in East St. Louis was held up by four people with guns who escaped in a car driven by a fifth person. All the players' funds and a safe were confiscated. The estimated take was $30,000. Mulepole commented, "The boys from St. Louis came over for a donation, and we gave it to them."

In the late 1920s and early 1930s, kidnapping of gamblers became an issue, and Mulepole was no exception. In 1931, the *St. Louis Post-Dispatch* reported that Mulepole supposedly paid a ransom of $35,000 after being kidnapped.

During 1937, Fritz operated a casino at 353 East Broadway, where he had three dice tables, including one reported as the largest in the Midwest, along with a handbook. A cigar store separated the two operations. Mulepole also instituted an automobile service that transported customers from downtown St. Louis and its principal hotels on the west side of the Eads Bridge to his establishment in downtown East St. Louis.

Roy "Colonel" Bowman

Roy Bowman was Adam Fritz's contemporary and competitor. No known pictures are available of Roy, but his World War I draft registration identified him as having light hair and gray eyes and being of medium height and stout build. Roy became known as the "Colonel" and the squarest gambler of them all in the area. He rose to become a kingpin and operated as a betting commissioner.

Roy was born in March 1878 at Bismarck, Missouri. He moved to Pilot Knob, Missouri, and in 1900 resided in Murphysboro, Illinois, with his mother. He married Margaret Reed from nearby Vienna, Illinois. Roy listed his occupation as a lather when he and Margaret found their way to East St. Louis. Shortly after the move, two sons were born, Roy Jr. in 1905 and Ira in 1908.

It only took until 1911 for Roy Sr. to make the papers. The St. Clair County sheriff raided a poker game operated by Roy at a tavern in East St. Louis. There were several players, one being the police commissioner of East St. Louis. On the table was $1,500 (about $48,000 in 2023). Roy took the funds with him and used them to pay everyone's fines: $100 for Roy and $50 each for the others.

In 1912, he was fined again for frequenting a gambling house, then he was arrested for vagrancy. Roy seemed to have some issues with the police and proceeded to sue them for the vagrancy charge. It was reported that Roy had properties in East Louis valued at $10,000 and properties in St. Clair County valued at $70,000. That equates to about $2.5 million today. The charges were dropped.

By 1920, Roy found his way to 107 Missouri Avenue in the vicinity of where Adam Fritz had been located. Roy stayed out of the papers until 1925, when he paid a $300 fine for keeping a gambling house. He shortly after found his way to 320 East Broadway and established a handbook and table games. This operation initially began with the time-honored cigar store as a front. Fritz had moved to 353 East Broadway, where his dice games and handbook flourished with a cigar store also separating the two operations.

The Colonel passed away in 1937. His sons Roy Jr. and Ira continued the operation on East Broadway. For a time, Ira shared ownership of the betting establishment, but he severed ties in the 1940s. Roy Jr. then set out to expand operations and opened a tavern and restaurant as a front for his activities at 318 East Broadway.

Fifteen other handbooks and six dice games were operating in East St. Louis during this period, all with the knowledge of the East St. Louis police. Fritz's and Roy's places were by far the largest and most important in terms of handbook operations, with the size and ability to pay off and lay out large bets from the other handbooks. Crowds streamed into these places from all over East St. Louis and southwest Illinois, but its biggest draw came from St. Louis.

The Bowman brothers maintained their father's kingpin reputation with their combination high-end tavern and restaurant, adjacent building for gambling and handbook and separate spot for the ladies if they wanted. Of course, all had air-conditioning, which was considered high status in the 1930s and 1940s.

Vic Doyle

Vic Doyle entered Adam Fritz's and Roy Bowman's area of operations after Prohibition ended in 1933. Vic, the oldest of nine children, started out learning to make cigars in a cigar factory in East St. Louis, then moved on to operating a dice game with Bill Gorman in 1929. He then opened a tavern and restaurant, Ringside Café, after Prohibition. The establishment opened at 315 Missouri Avenue, a stone's throw from East St. Louis police headquarters.

Vincent Harold Doyle, the author's uncle, created the East Side's Ringside Casino. In the 1940s, it was the largest gambling establishment in the Midwest. *Doyle family photo, circa 1940.*

From around 1936 to 1947, East St. Louis had nine different handbooks operating in the city, with five more operating in Belleville and a few more in Madison County in Granite City, Venice and Madison. The largest handbooks of the group could be found in East St. Louis at Fritz's and Bowman's places on Broadway. But a third competitor, Vic Doyle's Ringside on Missouri Avenue, rose to their level and then passed them. Doyle became the kingpin of casino operations as well as bookmaking.

Vic's operation grew to become known simply as Ringside. It expanded further and came to be called Ringside Casino, which included a handbook at 319 Missouri Avenue. In 1942 and 1943, that location was considered the largest gambling house in the Midwest. Vic opened a new, larger Ringside Casino operation in 1944 at 110 West Broadway; the handbook stayed on Missouri Avenue. The West Broadway spot was located at the foot of the Eads Bridge. Free transportation from downtown St. Louis and on-site parking were provided for customers.

As the Ringside grew to become the largest gambling operation in southern Illinois and then the Midwest, Vic became the kingpin and known as a "gambling impresario." Stories abounded about the Ringside's goings-on, and newspapers provided vivid descriptions of its location and operations.

Jim Doyle

James Joseph Doyle, the author's uncle and namesake was Vic Doyle's brother and ran the Ringside Casino's handbook operation. *Doyle family photo, circa 1943.*

The Ringside was a family operation. Vic's brother Jim Doyle joined in with his specialty, bookmaking. Their original operation became the Ringside Café, a tavern with typical gaming operations, which was a specialty of Vic's. The brothers also created a handbook, which was Jim's specialty.

Jim had a different path to the gambling business. Like others in the family, he worked at the stockyards in his younger days, first as a cattle driver and then as a cattle buyer. Jim, part of a large Irish Catholic family, was born in 1899, the fifth child and fourth son. At one time, he considered a call to the priesthood. Jim went to the seminary at St. Henry's in Belleville and finished three years of college. But something changed him, and he found a different calling. Jim married Viola Dinan in 1925; they had no children.

TWO EAST SIDE BANDITS SEIZE $1,500 IN STREET

A robber band had been credited today by the East St. Louis police with its second big holdup in three days. The second robbery was committed in the heart of downtown East St. Louis at 6:15 o'clock last night when two armed men seized a pouch containing $1,500 from two employes of a racing handbook shop and escaped in an automobile driven by a third man.

The men robbed were Edward Costello and James Doyle, employed in the handbook shop operated by Vic Doyle, brother of James, at 315 Missouri avenue. The holdup occurred in front of 321 Missouri avenue as Costello and Doyle were on their way to the night depository of the First National Bank of East St. Louis, a block away.

The two armed robbers answered the description of two bandits who held up the Circle Packing Co., 319 Winstanley avenue, at 3:15 p. m. Saturday, escaping with $3,100 in cash and $1,400 in checks.

Left: An article describing James Doyle being robbed of handbook receipts. The amount was about $18,000 in today's terms. St. Louis Star Times, *February 25, 1936*.

Right: Handbook operation at the Ringside Casino. St. Louis Post-Dispatch, *June 18, 1944*.

For the 1920 Census, Jim listed his occupation as a cattle buyer. For the 1930 Census, he listed himself as a bookkeeper at a poolroom. In 1936, it was reported that Jim was robbed at gunpoint on the way to First National Bank on Missouri Avenue. He admitted to carrying daily receipts from the Ringside handbook in the amount of $1,500 (about $32,000 today). In 1940, he identified himself as a clerk at a cigar store and listed his income as $3,000. Such comparisons of income and occupation would raise eyebrows if they had been made public at the time.

Jim, like Adam Fritz, was not immune to his handbook receipts being taken.

Business really picked up beginning in 1936. Deposits at the same bank started being handled differently, with police in many instances assuring no more holdups.

Casino operation at the Ringside Casino. St. Louis Post-Dispatch, *June 18, 1944.*

Four years later, in 1940, the Ringside's bookmaking establishment was estimated to be drawing between two hundred and four hundred patrons daily, many of whom were women, a rarity. The patrons were accommodated by a thirty-foot-long counter with twelve clerks assisting. Gross annual income for Ringside was placed at between $400,000 and $500,000. The net profit would have been between 10 and 12 percent of gross income (between $5 million and $6 million today).

As a service to the bettors, Ringside also contained what was commonly referred to as a lunch counter. This became the specialty of the youngest brother, Ray, my father. My dad was not around for all the prosperous years. He told me that he ran the concession stand at the Ringside, which basically included all types of food items, along with tobacco, candy, newspapers and other items that the bettors might find appealing. My dad left the Ringside for the army in 1942 and at same time married Virginia Burgoon, my mom. By 1944, he was on a ship destined for Marseilles, France, and by May 1945, he was marching into Munich, Germany. Jim passed away in 1945 while Ray was moving through Germany. Ray came back to the East Side at the end of 1945. He found the Ringside at a new location. He and my mom welcomed me and then my sister Kathy.

During this time, Ringside Casino was identified as a palatial gambling house. Dice, poker, blackjack and roulette were the favorites, along with other choices. The nightly gross was estimated at $100,000 (about $5 million in 2023). The Ringside had about one hundred people on the payroll, and their collective daily pay was estimated at $1,500. High rollers found their way to the Ringside. A businessman from Alton supposedly lost $90,000 at the dice tables in one night. The Broadway location became so successful that a new, luxurious restaurant and entertainment venue called Bush's Steak House opened next door.

East St. Louis Politics

In 1938, Patrick Coomey, head of the board of assessors, wasn't concerned about the legality of gambling. He was more interested in assessing the establishments at their fair-market value and taxing them accordingly. Vic's Ringside in 1938 was assessed at a rate that resulted in a tax of $16 ($330 today). Coomey determined that the assessed value of the Ringside should have been $175,000. At a rate of 40 percent of the assessed value, that would have been a tax of $70,000. Coomey did not make much headway with this proposition.

East St. Louis, given its increasing population and the expansion of nearby major employers, saw gambling flourish. At the same time, St. Louis saw economic and population gains. The city's thriving downtown business district was within easy access to downtown East St. Louis and its gambling operations. A major distinction between the two locales was that the East Side maintained late hours for its entertainment venues, including bars, restaurants and gambling operations. And East Side politicians were on board for these operations. St. Louis, on the other hand, kept a firmer grip on things. Gambling existed, but not to the level and openness of the East Side. Additionally, bars and restaurants in St. Louis could not stay open late, and they were required to be closed on Sunday. Traffic jams across the Eads Bridge to the East Side became common on the weekends.

Starting after the repeal of Prohibition in 1933 and up to 1947, government authorities directly overseeing the community were on board with gambling operations that cooperated with them. Not everyone in Illinois was happy about this, but the East St. Louis political hierarchy was almost completely on board. The increase in industrial facilities and World War II production helped to create what today would look like something on the Las Vegas Strip.

Unlike at the Las Vegas Strip, the casinos in East St. Louis operated separately from entertainment activities, which were located apart from them and did not operate at the same level. There were plenty of entertainment choices on downtown streets, just not at the casinos.

Just outside the casino doors on Broadway, Collinsville and Missouri Avenues could be found places such as the Canadian Club, the Terrace, Johnny Perkins's Palladium, the Tom Tom Club, Hammers Café, Keifleins, the O/B Café, Page's Café and the Broadway Café. Restaurants, bars,

The Majestic Theater opened in 1928 and enjoyed tremendous success until closing in the 1960s. It was placed in the National Register of Historic Places in 1985. It is shown here in a circa 1920s postcard. *Institute for Urban Research.*

live entertainment and other Vegas-type offerings could be found in these and other places until the early morning hours. The Majestic Theater, an elaborate stage and movie house, was also there.

In the 1930s, dice games, bookmaking and other activities could be found on the 300 and 400 blocks of Missouri Avenue and on the 300 block of Broadway. Broadway continues to be the gateway street to the Missouri side, with direct Eads Bridge access to Washington Avenue in downtown St. Louis.

Mulepole Fritz's establishments did not have the cachet that the Ringside had. By the 1940s, bookmaking had become Fritz's main business, which was considerable. In 1936, his place at 353 East Broadway consisted of a cigar store in front and, behind it, a handbook consisting of a fifty-foot blackboard with racing results, betting windows and one hundred chairs for bettors. A second room behind that held two large dice tables and a pool table. By 1939, Fritz was accommodating about three hundred patrons daily.

Fritz changed locations for his operations. He stayed at 353 East Broadway and then bought additional buildings at 413–15 Missouri Avenue to hold his expanded bookmaking operations. He remodeled the buildings at a cost of $50,000 ($5.5 million in 2023). When remodeling the Missouri Avenue building in 1939, Fritz paid $8,000 for an air-conditioner to be installed.

East Side Decline

Times have changed, and St. Louis and East St. Louis are not the same. But one thing has remained. Gambling still exists on the East Side and three kingpins, in different operating forms—Casino Queen Casino and Bookmaking, Fairmont Racetrack and Bookmaker and Alton Belle Casino and Bookmaker—continue to draw St. Louisans to Illinois, where casinos and handbooks are fully legal and operating at significant levels. Mulepole, Roy and Vic would be happy to see it all.

Vic Doyle and Mulepole Fritz endured numerous bombings, at both the Ringside on Missouri Avenue and Fritz's establishment on Broadway. In 1943 alone, Fritz endured four bombings and Vic experienced three. Their code was to not report these and to avoid police intervention. During a 1938 incident, when Vic's brother Jim was questioned by a reporter regarding what had happened, Jim merely said that "a boiler exploded by accident." These kingpins sustained and maintained their businesses throughout all of these incidents and saw growth and prosperity.

The same level of bombing was endured by Mont Tennes in 1907 in Chicago. He stayed with it and opened a new casino and grew his wire service. The Doyles and Fritz followed in Tennes's footsteps some forty years later. Tennes had rebounded from bombings with different operations, and Vic and Mulepole followed that plan. Capone's group started interfering with Mont's handbooks, and he stepped aside in 1927, closing his casinos and handbooks, then selling his wire service interest to Mo Annenberg.

Vic Doyle was one of the first to recognize the influence of Al Capone's outfit with Buster Wortman's invasion of the East Side and the Capone outfit's monopoly of the Pioneer Wire Service. Vic then closed the Ringside Casino when the Capone outfit started cutting in on its profits.

A similar set of events happened to Mont Tennes going up against the Capone mob in Chicago some twenty years before the bombings of the Ringside. Uncle Vic stepped aside from the casino and handbook operation; interferences were all overseen by the wire service monopoly, now in the hands of the Capone group. Vic paid for protection, as Mont had, but that got to be too much, and Vic stepped aside.

Age, changing population, changing city conditions and organized crime probably would have also played a role in Vic's and Mulepole's, stepping away in 1947.

Indicted For Malfeasance In Gambling Probe

George V. Gruenewald,
Ex-Sheriff Of St. Clair County

John T. Connors,
Mayor Of East St. Louis

John T. English,
East St. Louis Commissioner

Albert P. Lauman.
East St. Louis Commissioner

Joseph Ganschinietz,
East St. Louis Commissioner

Leo J. Dougherty,
Resigned Commissioner Of
East St. Louis

Article showing "Indictment for Political Malfeasance" of East St. Louis government office holders. Belleville News Democrat, *May 12, 1947*.

POLITICAL CORRUPTION

The mayor of St. Louis in 1947, Aloys Kaufmann, said the East Side area was a "corrupt and lawless conglomeration of communities." How true that turned out to be.

An example of this can be found in a 1939 interview with the *St. Louis Star and Times*. A reporter with the third-largest newspaper of St. Louis pointed out to the mayor of East St. Louis, John T. Connors, that handbooks were operating in the open there. Police closed the bookie shops in St. Louis, and patrons were going to East St. Louis shops to make bets. The reporter asked the mayor what he was going to do about closing the handbooks. Connors, who was also the police commissioner at the time, said, "We'll take care of our own business in East St. Louis." No further comments were made. The statement by the chief prosecutorial official of St. Clair County was that he only prosecuted; the handbook situation was Mayor Connors's responsibility.

By 1947, things had begun to change. The following politicians were indicted for malfeasance in office: John T. Connors, mayor; John T. English, police commissioner; George Gruenewald, sheriff; Albert Lauman, fire commissioner; Joseph Ganschinietz, finance commissioner; Leo Dougherty, street commissioner; and Robert Sweeny, a police inspector. Vic Doyle, Adam Fritz and Roy Bowman were indicted for gambling. The politicians, and the ones before them, made sure gambling stayed in place for many years.

Predictably, all the indictments were dismissed. Despite this, things did change. The indictments put an end to the open gambling that had been operating for many years. East St. Louis's economy began to change, and World War II veterans were looking for housing and began to move away from downtown. The same went on in St. Louis. The other factor was the growth of the Capone gang's influence in the area. It controlled wire services and demanded a share in all gambling operators' casino proceeds.

20

OPEN GAMBLING IN NEW ORLEANS

1930s-1950

The same pattern of wide-open gambling seen in East St. Louis was also found in New Orleans between the 1930s and 1950. During the 1900–50 period, New Orleans did not have a population comparable to that of New York, Philadelphia and St. Louis. But the history and acceptance of gambling placed the city and the state of Louisiana at the top of the gaming industry.

History of Louisiana Gambling

Louisiana's French founders built a number of cabarets and billiard halls in New Orleans, even before a church was erected. After the completion of St. Louis Church in 1727 (now known as St. Louis Cathedral), some residents continued to gamble rather than attend Mass. In the eighteenth century, Louisiana officials passed ordinances outlawing gambling and other activities considered vices during religious services, limited the pots for games of chance and finally prohibited gambling altogether. When none of these measures proved successful, Louisiana governor Louis Billouart de Kerlérec opened a government-run casino in New Orleans in 1753. All efforts to curb gambling failed, and it remained prevalent decades after Spain took control of the colony following the French and Indian War (1754–63).

Fairgrounds Track, New Orleans, circa 1920. *fairgroundsracecourse.com.*

In 1803, when Louisiana became a U.S. territory, New Orleans had more gambling venues than New York, Philadelphia, Boston and Baltimore combined. So entrenched was the practice that when the federal government banned gambling in the territory in 1812, it exempted New Orleans. After statehood, Louisiana swung back and forth between extremes—legalizing casinos and banning them—though these efforts had a limited effect on the number of facilities. The state authorized six operations for New Orleans in 1823. In 1827, New Orleans opened the first twenty-four-hour full-service casino in the country. The state again legalized gambling in the city after the Civil War (1861–65).

Horse racing also played a major role in the changing betting environment in New Orleans. In fact, Fairgrounds Track is the third-oldest track in the United States, after Freehold in New Jersey and Saratoga Springs in New York.

In the 1920s, legal pari-mutuel betting on horse races at the New Orleans Fair Grounds became the only officially sanctioned form of gambling in the state. It continues in operation today and is owned by Business Corporation of Churchill Downs Racetrack in Louisville.

Gambling in New Orleans

Tom Shaw began his gambling career at Crescent Hall, a billiards room and gambling spot in New Orleans at the intersection of Canal Street and St. Charles Avenue. In 1940, Crescent Hall was still operating at the same intersection.

Illegal casinos continued to operate, as the state alternated between raiding gambling sites and ignoring them. It was similar to how East Side

Left: Crescent Hall, New Orleans, on the corner of Canal and St. Charles, circa 1940. *New Orleans History Project.*

Right: The O'Dwyer brothers in straw hats, circa 1940s. They were the major gambling operators in Jefferson Parish from 1916 until the mid-1950s. *New Orleans History Project.*

gambling operated in the open from the 1920s to 1940s. There were several establishments, but a significant concentration was located in Jefferson Parish, just a few miles from the French Quarter and downtown New Orleans. Political cooperation with gambling kingpins, as in the East Side, was seen in Jefferson Parish. Mayor Connors approved of gambling in Illinois, and Jefferson Parish had a sheriff named Frank Clancy. Sheriff Clancy, for a price, made sure the gambling houses remained open. He did this from 1928 to 1956, when he finally failed to be reelected.

The Louisiana gambling houses contained roulette wheels, card games and keno operations. Bookmakers could also be found there but were more spread out and did not operate at the same level as in the East Side. Many were in the suburbs of Jefferson Parish, adjoining Orleans Parish. Such locations were scattered and operated in a wide-open way. Limousines were provided by the establishments to bring patrons coming off the streetcar. The popular places were O'Dwyer's, Original Club, Forest, Chesterfield Club, Original Southport Club and New Southport Club.

These sites were operated by individual owners who were well known and respected in the community. Like my Uncle Vic and Jim Doyle, operators in Jefferson were the O'Dwyer brothers George and Rudy. Their family operated gambling sites from 1916 to 1942, when their original club burned down. They then began other operations, which continued into the 1950s.

Contrary to the East Side, a redeeming feature for some of these enterprises was food. New Orleans, being a gourmet city, had a solid food-

Left: Frank Clancy, sheriff of Jefferson Parish, made sure gambling remained open from 1928 to 1956. New Orleans Louisiana Weekly, *January 7, 1956.*

Right: Carlos Marcello. New York's organized crime kingpin. In New Orleans, he oversaw taking over gambling operations from the independent operators. Shreveport Times, *March 24, 1959.*

Opposite: An advertisement for O'Dwyer's place on Jefferson Highway, circa 1956. *New Orleans History Project.*

loving scene to go along with the gambling. Among the places that remained open were supper clubs, which had dining facilities in a building, usually a house that contained gaming facilities. This is similar to what Roy Bowman was trying to do in the East Side. If a raid closed gambling in such a house, it closed, and the dining facility remained open.

The Kefauver hearings placed a damper on New Orleans gambling, as it did in the East Side. Namely, the gambling houses were owned and operated by individuals who were well respected. These operations were smaller than those found in the East Side but were numerous and well attended. Starting in about the same 1947–50 period, organized crime worked its way into the gambling houses of New Orleans, causing their closure and/or resulting in owners leaving the business. Some operators tried smaller underground ventures or associated with organized crime.

In 1947, Carlos Marcello of New Orleans began the takeover. He operated as a representative of Frank Costello, the head of New York's criminal organization.

Gambling didn't disappear. But ownership and the method of operation between the 1920s and 1940s changed. The same level of individual operations essentially disappeared. Many in New Orleans took the Kefauver hearings seriously and had the small gambling houses closed down. There were efforts at underground operations, with the majority of them falling under the influence of organized crime.

New Orleans Gambling Today

As in other states, including Illinois, Louisiana underwent economic downturns and revenue declines. Only the collapse of the state's oil-based economy in the early 1980s prompted the expansion of legalized gambling. Louisiana's voters approved an amendment that allowed the return of a lottery in September 1991.

Five years after Congress passed the Indian Gaming Regulatory Act in 1988, the three Native American tribes in Louisiana recognized by the federal government—the Chitimachas, Coushattas and Tunica-Biloxis—negotiated compacts with the state to open land-based casinos. After gaining recognition, the Jena Band of Choctaws negotiated a compact with

Governor Murphy Foster Jr. in 2002. The federal government approved the first agreements, and these tribes continue to operate land-based casinos. The Jena Band of Choctaws, however, never gained federal approval. Proposing a casino site near Lake Charles, the Jena faced opposition from both Texans and Coushattas, each group fearing that the new casino would lure customers from their establishments.

With casinos authorized in nearby Mississippi in 1991, the promise of increased revenues combined with the prospect of new jobs convinced the Louisiana legislature to approve fifteen riverboat casinos, five in Shreveport–Bossier City, four in Lake Charles, three in New Orleans and three in Baton Rouge. The same year, the governor allowed the legalization of video poker machines to become law without his signature. (These machines had operated illegally in bars and restaurants since the 1980s.) In Illinois, ten riverboat casinos were authorized. Louisiana, with more water outlets, approved fifteen. Eventually, legislation authorizing construction of a casino in New Orleans was enacted. The casino opened at the same Crescent Hall intersection of Canal and St. Charles.

Legal gambling continued to expand as racetracks lobbied for slot machines. Their efforts eventually proved successful, and machines were installed on three tracks in 1997 and at a fourth track a few years later. Video poker also spread across the state as businesses took advantage of the legislature's inclusion of "truck stops," which it failed to clearly define.

In New Orleans and throughout the state of Louisiana, legalized gambling has played an important cultural, political and economic role from the colonial era to the present. Now part of the Louisiana landscape, gambling attracts tourists, provides jobs and produces revenue—more than $723 million in direct revenue in fiscal year 2008–9. Currently, more than twenty casinos operate in the state, including thirteen on riverboats and four

Harrah's Casino, New Orleans, on the corner of Canal and St. Charles, circa 2010. *Harrah's Casino brochure.*

on racetracks. In addition, residents and visitors can play video poker in bars, restaurants and truck stops throughout southern Louisiana. Casinos on tribal lands have become an important source of income for many of the state's Native Americans. In addition, sports betting was authorized throughout the state in January 2021 and began operating in October of that year. In January 2023, $280 million was wagered during that month. Both physical locations and online betting are in operation.

Sports betting continues to expand with Caesars' physical location at Harrah's Casino and FanDuel at the now land-based riverboat casino Treasure Chest in Kenner. Fairgrounds Track is still in operation and includes the Twin Spires sports book.

21

ORGANIZED CRIME

During their operating days of the 1930s and 1940s, Vic Doyle, Mulepole Fritz and Roy Bowman were bombed, threatened, kidnapped and indicted. Yet thanks to the cooperation of police and politicians, they managed to keep, for the most part, criminal elements from the gambling operations for extended periods of time. Eventually, organized crime did take a foothold, and this spelled the end of large-scale, independent gambling operations.

Organized crime began operating in the United States before the 1940s. The most impactful crime group in East St. Louis was Al Capone's outfit from Chicago. Southern Illinois had its own well-known outlaws, the Shelton Gang. On the Missouri side, the criminal gang Egan's Rats were the tyrants.

The largest group, one that created modern organized crime in the United States, came from New York. Among its well-known names were Charles Luciano and Meyer Lansky. Lucky Luciano created the foundation of the Five Families that operated in New York City and then expanded across the country. Lansky was the accountant and financial wizard who oversaw the organization. Luciano headed a crime family in New York but exerted his influence over all the families and extended it nationally. Lansky accounted for all activities regardless of location. Frank Costello took over the New York operations after Luciano left the country.

Lansky had a close associate named Benjamin Siegel, better known as Bugsy, who ran gambling and bootlegging operations in New York. He ran other illicit activities, including overseeing Murder, Inc. Around 1936,

Benjamin Siegel, seen here about 1944, was New York's organized crime representative. In taking over criminal operations, he established the beginning of Las Vegas and its style of gambling offerings. *gaminganddestinations.com*.

the Five Families sent Siegel to Los Angeles to expand their operations. Opposition from other crime organizations greeted Bugsy, but he resolved all resistance in gangland fashion.

It was reported that Siegel visited East St. Louis around 1946, and it is more than likely that he took some of the positive things found at the Ringside with him to Las Vegas. In fact, during the beginning of the creation of Las Vegas, several dealers and workers from the Ringside went to work at the casinos opening in Vegas, including the Riviera, the Dunes and other places that began in the late 1940s and early 1950s.

The East St. Louis police had its own enforcer, Inspector Robert Sweeney, to make sure no gang-related interference came to its citizens, particularly to gambling operators. Sweeney was told that Siegel was at a Missouri Avenue spot, and he went to see him. Sweeney confronted the gangster, telling him, "You have one minute to get outta here and cross the bridge back to St. Louis." Siegel left right away without incident. For what it's worth, Sweeney had a quick trigger finger.

With all the cash flowing through the Ringside and Bowman's establishment, Vic and Roy wanted to make sure their receipts were deposited in the bank. Inspector Sweeney's son Robert "Tree" Sweeney, in his writings, relates that his Dad would take him to school every morning, then stop by Vic's and Roy's places and pick up leather briefcases containing receipts from the day before. They were then delivered to First National Bank on Missouri Avenue. No one ever tried to rob him.

Tree Sweeney relates that his dad spent a half hour every day cleaning and polishing his Smith & Wesson and eyeballed every bullet for defects.

POLICE INSPECTOR
ROBERT SWEENEY

Police Guard for Gambling House 'Bankroll'

—By a Post-Dispatch Staff Photographer.
East St. Louis police guarding the "bankroll" of the Ringside gambling establishment on the East Side. The black Packard, parked with wheels away from curb, is being entered by R. EMMETT FARRELL, partner in the Ringside, who is carrying a "bankroll" of approximately $65,000 to cover one day's play. Following Farrell on sidewalk is former East St. Louis City Detective RAY CASHEL, now a private guard. In the left foreground, parked double, is the automobile of Police Inspector Robert Sweeney of the East St. Louis Police Department.

Left: Inspector Robert Sweeney of East St. Louis. He was the enforcer in keeping East Louis free of organized crime and protecting gambling operations. St. Louis Post-Dispatch, *April 16, 1947.*

Right: This image shows East St. Louis Inspector Sweeney serving as a guard for the Ringside Casino deposits; the money shown would be $3 million today. St. Louis Post-Dispatch, *September 13, 1946.*

Inspector Sweeney was widely known for the number of shoot-outs and deaths he was responsible for. His method of enforcement was to keep a list of individuals he did not want within the limits of East St. Louis on his shift, and he made sure they left if he found them. This included members of the Shelton gang and Buster Wortman.

The Ringside bankroll stated in the accompanying image from 1946 is listed at $65,000 for one day's play (about $3 million today). This was not for a weekend night, but for a Thursday. Saturday's play would more than likely have been much higher.

During this time, Siegel, who had become something of a celebrity with Hollywood types, was running secluded gambling activities around Los Angeles and on offshore gambling ships. Local politicians and police were not as benevolent in their acceptance of open gambling as had been the case in East St. Louis. Siegel noticed that gambling was legal in Las Vegas, a relatively short distance from Los Angeles. A hotel in Vegas was under construction at the time, and $1 million had already been put into it, but it was not finished, and the developers ran out of money.

Siegel talked Luciano and Lansky into taking it over, calling it the Flamingo. They needed about $1 million to finish construction. One year and some months later, Flamingo opened at a total cost of $6 million (about $79 million today). Unfortunately, at the hotel's opening, unusually heavy rains kept the expected crowds away, and a high roller got lucky and won $300,000 within a couple of days. Siegel eventually got his Hollywood friends to show up, signed top entertainers and basically became the driving force in developing what is now the Las Vegas Strip.

Back in Illinois, the East Side's gambling establishments changed with the building and expansion of the Las Vegas Strip and its multiple choices of gaming spots and entertainment.

Siegel knew there had to be something other than gambling to get the crowds to the desert. He started hiring well-known entertainers to play Vegas, a tradition that continues to this day. East St. Louis casinos had enough on their hands, with entertainment being provided near the casinos but not owned by them. The East Side was not in a desert, but it had to deal with all four seasons and their high humidity, cold, snow and rainstorms. Illinois casinos also had to deal with bombings, political payoffs and enforcement of what generally were honest, profitable operations run by individual business owners.

Bugsy Siegel met his demise in a gangland shooting in 1947. He never saw how much of his vision had become a reality.

East Side Criminal Takeover

Like Carlos Marcello's tenure in New Orleans, organized crime came to the East Side at this time. Instead of New York interests, Al Capone's Chicago mob arrived, with Frank Wortman as its representative.

Buster Wortman, born in 1904, was the son of an East St. Louis fire captain but spent his early years in North St. Louis. He turned to crime in his late teens. By 1926, he had begun running errands for the bootlegging Shelton brothers of southern Illinois and by the early 1930s was acting as an enforcer for the Sheltons. At one of the brothers' distilleries in 1933, a federal agent was beaten. Buster wound up in Leavenworth from 1934 to 1941. Following his release, he organized an army of gunmen to drive the Sheltons from the region.

At the same time, Buster affiliated with the Chicago-based Capone syndicate. He went to work to create a virtual monopoly on gambling, including slot machines, pinball machines, handbooks, craps, and card games. One of his major methods of gaining control was in the squeeze that ended the Continental News Service, after which Buster gained control of the wire service for bookies. He wound up charging bookies for the service, between $3 and $150 per week per phone. Wortman also demanded 40 percent of the daily take of each handbook. The Chicago Crime Commission in 1950 pointed out that Wortman's group in the East Side were also paying financial homage to Frank Costello, head of the national syndicate, taking over from Lucky Luciano.

Frank "Buster" Wortman was Chicago's organized crime representative in the East Side and St. Louis. He was responsible for the elimination of independent gambling operators. St. Louis Globe-Democrat, January 12, 1960.

In the 1920s, the Shelton Gang dictated what bootleg whiskey East Siders drank. By 1947, Wortman and the Capone outfit had started to dictate who would be making a profit from gambling on the East Side.

The established independent, big-time gamblers such as Adam Fritz and Vic Doyle decided to not be a part of this and went on to other ventures. In their place, small, independent bookies began operating in the back rooms of taverns. There were four such bookies on the East Side who subscribed to the Pioneer Wire Service.

By 1950, the nearby town of Granite City had moved to shut down all handbooks in an effort to stop Wortman's group from entering the area. Operators of the Hyde Park Club in nearby Venice, Illinois, closed their casino in 1949 rather than operate it for Wortman's benefit.

The East St. Louis city administration, in its usual operating style, told reporters that they were not very worried about things, as Buster Wortman let them know he would not tolerate major criminals operating on the East Side. He wanted to keep down any "heat" from the newspapers.

22

KEFAUVER HEARINGS

CRIMINAL IMPACT ON GAMBLING

While the Capone group was gaining a foothold on the East Side, organized crime takeovers were being felt in major cities across the United States. Gambling was a prime candidate for takeover, facilitated by the monopoly of wire services and the protection racket of the casinos. Other industries were also targets, as were labor unions. As with previous such criminal infiltration, political cooperation and corruption was a necessary ingredient.

As criminal activity spread throughout the nation, of particular concern was the evolution of Las Vegas and the concentration of organized crime. Many cities and states called for federal help in dealing with organized crime, but the U.S. government had few mechanisms to tackle the problem. The biggest concern at the time was interstate commerce and related concerns of labor racketeering holding the economy hostage.

As a result, on January 5, 1950, Senator Estes Kefauver of Tennessee introduced a resolution to investigate organized crime's role in interstate commerce. By May, the Special Committee to Investigate Crime in Interstate Commerce had been established. This became known as the Kefauver Committee, and it held hearings in fourteen major cities. The hearings were broadcast live on television.

All of the major known organized crime figures were subpoenaed to appear at the various hearing sites. Several appeared, and several refused. Those who didn't appear as requested were acquitted of any wrongdoing.

Senator Estes Kefauver (standing) is shown with other members of the Kefauver Committee. It officially began as the United States Senate's Special Committee to Investigate Crime in Interstate Commerce. *mafiahistory.us.*

Also subpoenaed were those identified as crooked law officers. It was made clear at the hearings that since 1927, there had been very little time that wide-open, commercialized gambling had not been tolerated by elected officials of St. Clair County and the cities within the county—of course, including East St. Louis.

The East Side's representative called to testify was Police Commissioner John T. English. He was from the same family that had opened Bush's Steak House next door to the Ringside Casino. He testified that he personally paid income taxes on $131,419 collected as treasurer for a Democratic political organization and were "political contributions" from 1943 to 1949. English declared that the money was not his. He began his public career in 1932; his commissioner salary was $4,000 a year. He didn't know what he was worth, he told the committee, but it requested that he furnish the information. He was told he could get a refund, but he refused.

Television was in its infancy at the time, but the broadcasts drew a large number of viewers. It meant big business for taverns and other social places that had television sets, allowing patrons to watch. The hearings were held in multiple cities, but the hearings in Washington, D.C., in the Senate were of particular importance.

By 1950, the U.S. population had reached 150 million, double that in 1900. It was reported that over 30 million people tuned in to watch the proceedings in March 1951. Additionally, it was reported that 72 percent of the country was familiar with the committee's work. That translates to 108 million people. One of the most famous quotes from a whole slew of witnesses called to testify was, "I refuse to answer on the grounds that it might incriminate me." This became a much-repeated part of the American dialogue, heard in schools, churches and taverns.

The most significant outcome of the hearings with regard to gambling was that legislative proposals and state ballot referenda to legalize gambling went down to defeat over the next several years, in part due to the revelation of organized crime's involvement in the gambling industry.

The committee was the first to suggest that civil law be expanded to combat organized crime. The FBI set up a unit to investigate organized crime, and at the state and local level, more than seventy crime commissions were established. In 1970, federal legislation was passed to combat crime syndicates in the form of the Racketeer Influenced and Corrupt Organizations Act. Commonly referred to as the RICO Act, it has been used in a number of cases.

23

JAMES J. CAROLL

ODDSMAKER, KEFAUVER HEARINGS

The East Side was also represented in the Kefauver hearings by a major betting kingpin with a national following.

Appearing in a 1951 televised hearing in Washington was Jimmy Carroll. He initially refused to show up, then he arrived wearing sunglasses, not wanting his face to be shown. The same had been done by noted New York crime boss Frank Costello.

The committee argued that gambling was the backbone of gangs and that gangs profited from vice, extortion, kidnapping and murder. Carroll proposed that the Continental Press Service, the bookie race news source that the committee was trying to smash, be taken down and substituted by Western Union Telegraph for distribution of bookie news if gambling was legalized.

Carroll's testimony was highly notable for two significant reasons. First, he explained that gambling was a biological necessity and that it will always find a way to be legalized. It took some time, but it turns out that Carroll was spot-on. Second, he argued that the way to end gambling's worst evils was to legalize it. The horse player gets a lift from playing, he said. The sport answers all his of problems. The players thinks that, sooner or later, his figures will start to click and his troubles will be over. "Gambling," Carroll said, "is the quality that gives substance to people's dreams."

James Carroll was from St. Louis and operated cigar stores at Eighth and Chestnut Streets in downtown St. Louis in the same manner as Tom Kearney and Kid Becker had. When St. Louis politicians and police stepped up their

James J. Carroll succeeded Tom Kearney as St. Louis's national betting commissioner. His testimony of overseeing $20 million in bets in 1947 made him a major witness at the Kefauver hearings. St. Louis Post-Dispatch, *February 25, 1951.*

closures, he moved to the more favorable East Side. His shop for operations was on the second floor of a building at 318A Missouri Avenue in downtown East St. Louis, across from Vic Doyle's place at 319 Missouri. Throughout this time of upheaval, Carroll attempted to stay in the handbook business and overcame all roadblocks.

Jimmy was born in the Irish section of North St. Louis called Kerry Patch in 1887. He came from Irish immigrant parents who ran a saloon and grocery. He gravitated early to the gaming tables, even while attending St. Louis University. He was reported to be a voracious reader and teetotaler, was reserved and pleasant and shunned publicity.

He was a contemporary of Tom Kearney and loyal to him. He declined to compete with Kearney for winter book business. After Kearney's death in 1936 and until his own retirement from the bets in 1950, Carroll became the only betting commissioner in the country with sufficient courage and bankroll to risk full book prices for the Kentucky Derby. He operated in downtown St. Louis in the 1930s and until 1941, when raids became too frequent in the city. He then opened a handbook operation on the East Side, next to Vic Doyle's place.

Horse racing was the meat and potatoes of Carroll's business, but his odds-on heavyweight champion boxing bouts, baseball pennant races, World Series games and presidential races were in great demand locally and nationally.

Jimmy Carroll was knowledgeable about finances. He was recognized as an oddsmaker with a national reputation and one who handled layoff bets. He testified that he never received police protection and never discussed protection with police officials.

The amount of money flowing through his East Side operation was stunning. Regarding horse gambling, Carroll put the 1949 gross of his operation at $20 million (over $400 million today). He said the horse betting made a gross profit of about $750,000. Supposedly, Jimmy claimed he received only $110,000 for advice and financing portions of returns. That would still be over $2 million in 2023 terms.

The amount may have been embellished, but Western Union testified that Carroll's company handled more than $3 million in telegraphed bets for the East Side operation. Southwestern Bell Telephone collected $64,736 for a 1950 telephone bill at the handbook. That's quite a phone bill for any time.

Carroll stayed until all the phone and telegraph lines were removed from his East Side offices. He was called before the Kefauver hearings to testify about his income and operations. Once he was made aware of the 10 percent federal tax that was going into effect on his winnings, he quit. Other gaming operators experienced the same taxation and closed down.

After retirement, Carroll lived a quiet life with his wife, son and five sisters. After years of fighting the IRS over income tax issues, he was cleared and did not resume betting. He eventually settled with the IRS at a much smaller amount than was being asked. He died in 1967 at eighty years of age.

Presidential odds from James J. Carroll for the 1936 election. St. Louis Globe-Democrat, *October 18, 1936.*

24

GAMBLING RECOVERY

Most states stayed away from Carroll's recommendation to legalize gambling. Nevada, and especially Las Vegas, took advantage of the nation's lack of legalizing betting, maintaining the industry's legal status. As a result, the state and city underwent major expansions, with casinos and sports betting drawing large numbers of visitors. The trend continues to this day.

Things began to change in other states starting in the 1970s. Illinois became the first state to introduce a lottery, in 1975. By 1976, New Jersey had legalized casino gambling, restricting it to one spot, Atlantic City. The first legal casino outside Nevada opened in 1978. The Resorts Casino Hotel in Atlantic City, New Jersey, was the first to open; it remains in business today. There have been several cycles of openings and closing of casinos and hotels since that time. The present-day Borgata in Atlantic City is flourishing. Some speculate that this is due to its similarity to Las Vegas operations and their array of amenities.

Of course, in the 1920s and until 1939, when racetrack betting became legal again in New Jersey, Atlantic City was noted for its open array of casinos and bookmaking, much like the East Side.

In 1970, horse-race betting remained popular in New York State, with bets being placed at the racetracks themselves. But there was also a lot of illegal betting taking place away from the tracks. New York legalized off-track betting, allowing betting shops to operate within the state. This was an attempt to legalize and regulate the betting industry, which had become associated with criminal activity, spotlighted by the Kefauver hearings.

Resorts Casino Hotel in Atlantic City, New Jersey, opened in 1978 as the first legal casino outside Nevada. *Skyscraper.com. CC-BY-SA-3.0.*

Lotteries were popular in New York from the time it was founded until the mid-1800s, when the activity was outlawed. It took until the 1960s for the state to reintroduce lotteries. New York is among the states with the most lottery sales.

A racino—a cross between a racetrack and a casino—allows punters to enjoy betting on horses and play games like slots and poker at video terminals. The New York legislature approved video lottery terminal gambling at racetracks in 2001. The first of these establishments launched in 2004, and there are now nine racinos operating across the state. Patrons can enjoy betting along with a range of casino games. Many racinos also sell lottery tickets,

New York residents visited racinos or traveled to other states to enjoy more traditional casino gaming. With Atlantic City just a short trip down the coast, New Yorkers often visited the big casinos there for a short vacation before coming back home. New York State saw that it was missing out on potential tax revenue as a result.

In 2013, the state officially made casino gambling legal. This marked the conclusion of a protracted period of attempts to legalize in-person casino gaming. Before this, casino games had been limited to Indian reservations or casinos in neighboring states. The move allowed the state to collect much-needed tax revenue.

In 2018, the U.S. Supreme Court overturned the long-standing Professional and Amateur Sports Protection Act, giving individual states the right to regulate sports betting. New York soon joined the list of states allowing sports betting. In 2021, New York sports books were able to accept both online and in-person bets. At the moment, online casino gaming is still off the table in New York,

It took until 1990 for legal gambling to return to St. Louis. In the years before that, it was only available on the East Side. In 1989, Iowa was the first state to introduce riverboat gambling. Illinois followed in 1990 with the Riverboat Casino Act. Missouri began its quest in 1992 to establish gambling on the Mississippi and Missouri Rivers.

The Illinois act called for a maximum of ten riverboat casinos to be licensed throughout the state. Initially, the rules called for boats to be located on water and to cruise. But after a few years, the rules were changed, and the boats could remain stationary and close to water.

ALTON BELLE

The Alton Belle received the first gambling license issued in Illinois in modern times. It opened for business in 1991 on the Mississippi at downtown Alton, Illinois. William Cellini, originally from Springfield, oversaw the venture. He had a long tenure in Illinois politics and was well connected with state officials. But it still took a collection of individual investors who could pass the vetting process of the gaming board. One potential investor ran into trouble and went to an associate to take his place.

That associate was John Connors, from Belleville. He brought along his brother, Jimmy Connors, as another investor. Combined, they accounted for $4 million of the total $10 million invested to get the boat operation up and running. Jimmy Connors, a professional tennis player, held the number-one ranking for five years in a row. In 1991, at the time of the Alton Belle's opening, he was in the spotlight for making the semifinals of the U.S. Open at age thirty-nine.

The Connors brothers were originally from East St. Louis. Not only that, but their grandfather was John T. Connors. The former mayor of East St. Louis, he had voted in favor of legalizing gambling and maintained the wide-

Left: Alton Belle in 1991 received the first gambling license issued in Illinois in modern times. Initially, cruising on the water was mandatory for gambling boats. *Kansas City Star, April 17, 1994.*

Below: Today, the Alton Belle is known as Argosy and is docked in Alton, Illinois. *argosyalton.com.*

open nature of the East Side and allowed Jimmy Carroll and Vic Doyle to operate at the level they did.

In 1993, Alton Belle filed to create a public company, Argosy Gaming. The stock offering looked to raise $45 million, of which the Connors brothers would each control 10.4 percent of the total shares. They vacated their ownership around 1997, due to a series of issues influencing both of them. Solid returns were a key to Argosy's operation, both with its original monopoly and also with a second riverboat opening up. In November 2004, Argosy's Alton boat, along with others that it had acquired over the years, was sold to Penn National Gaming for $2.2 billion ($42 billion in 2023).

In 2023, Argosy finds itself still in operation as one of the few remaining riverboat casinos. It does not have any hotel facilities. The casino started with 296 slots and twenty-two table games. In 2023, there were 827 slots and twelve table games. An important addition was the inclusion of sports betting at the casino, with the Barstool betting operation. The casino expanded its facilities to offer 500 new and modern slots and nine table games in a new space. Compared to its rivals, it remains the smallest casino.

Casino Queen

The second riverboat to offer gambling, offering competition with the Alton Belle/Argosy, was the Casino Queen. Illinois politics played a role in its creation. It opened in 1993.

The backstory begins with Capone's group taking over and inheriting a declining operation in East St. Louis. A series of financially successful independent operations were in the economically prosperous community. That all began to change after World War II. Of course, the changing economic foundation of East St. Louis's industry, population movements and political culture also contributed. The city today is a shell of its former self, but one thing has survived to provide a boost to its economy: gambling.

Today, all of the Missouri Avenue buildings once occupied by East Side gambling activities no longer exist.

St. Louis native Yogi Berra once said, "It's déjà vu all over again." And that is the case for betting in the East Side. Today, there is a full-scale casino in the city, including a walk-up handbook for sports betting. It is the city's largest employer. The Casino Queen Casino and Sports Book is located at the Mississippi River, across the Eads Bridge from St. Louis.

This modern version of casinos on the East Side includes a hotel, multiple dining and bar facilities and rooms with views of the riverfront and the iconic Gateway Arch. Las Vegas has an ambiance and building footprint that makes it hard to duplicate. The East Side does attempt to provide the gambling amenities found in Las Vegas with a hint of the packaging of its venue. St. Louis also has a full-scale casino and hotel near the Eads Bridge. But no bookmaking (sports betting) is allowed.

In 1990, Illinois enacted a riverboat casino law authorizing licenses for ten casinos to open in the state. East St. Louis was the only city in Illinois guaranteed a casino license under the state's Distressed Cities Act. It then

The Casino Queen in East St. Louis received approval in 1993. Cruising was initially mandatory for operating. St. Louis Post-Dispatch, *April 24, 1994.*

became a question as to which group would win the right to be granted the license. In a somewhat typical Illinois political manner, the answer rested with Morton Friedman. He was executive director of the Illinois Gaming Board, the state's top gaming regulator. This was the agency that would issue the license.

The story goes that Gordon Bush, East St. Louis's mayor at the time, went to Friedman, asking for help in locating a casino on the riverfront. Friedman agreed and went to work on it. At the same time, Michael Gaughan, a veteran Las Vegas casino operator, wanted in on the action in Illinois. He was the son of a casino owner and ran the Barbery Coast and Gold Coast hotel and casino in Las Vegas. He was involved with a group to locate a casino in Moline. But then he met with Friedman, who told Gaughan to look at East Louis instead.

Friedman told him to meet with the Bidwill's, which at this time meant Charles Bidwill III, owner of Sportsman's Park racetrack. Charles would ultimately become chairman of the Casino Queen Board of Directors. Friedman then steered developer William Koman Sr. to Bidwill for a place on the Casino Queen team. Koman, in addition to being a St. Louis–based real estate developer, was a former professional football player. He had played with Baltimore and Philadelphia and, more important, spent his final eight years with the Chicago and St. Louis Cardinals, the team the Bidwill family owned in both cities.

Casino Queen 1994

The Casino Queen opened in June 1993, offering nine hundred jobs on a boat called *White Star One*. Craig Travers became the general manager. He had worked for Michael Gaughan at his Las Vegas casinos. Construction of the hotel began in 1998. The 157-room hotel opened in January 2000 at a cost of $15 million ($32 million today). Changed regulations led to the casino being moved inland. At the same time, the facility added ten thousand square feet of gaming space. The *White Star One* was sold for $600,000 in 2014. In addition to the hotel, an RV park is part of the property. The casino has 1,100 slots and thirty-four table games in its thirty-eight thousand square feet of gaming space.

Casino Queen Today

In 2012, Koman and his group sold the Casino Queen to an employee stock ownership plan (ESOP) for $170 million. To pay down its debt for the purchase, in 2014, the ESOP sold the real estate of the Casino Queen to Gaming and Leisure Properties Inc., a real estate investment trust specializing in casino properties, for $140 million. The ESOP then agreed to a lease back at a cost of $14 million per year. Current data is not available, but the Casino Queen has reported generating over $160 million for the City of East St. Louis between 1993 and 2009.

The methods of operation and offerings at casinos were established at the Ringside Casino and Las Vegas. The people, clothes, cars and jobs may be

The Casino Queen today is docked and has expanded. *casinoqueenstlouis.com*.

different, but the slot machines, blackjack games, roulette wheels, dice tables, baccarat tables and handbooks still flourish in their basics. Today, operations are truly in the open, like during the East Side's gambling days. Politicians have accepted gaming's legal status, likely a result of seeing the potential income stream.

Vic Doyle and Mulepole Fritz retreated into the real estate business. Fritz was the largest real estate tax lien buyer in St. Clair County, even before the decline of his gaming business. He bought up $500,000 in lines in 1940 alone. Fritz passed away in 1960 at age eighty-three, survived by his wife. His obituary identified him as a "betting commissioner." Vic Doyle got into real estate, also with commercial buildings. He bought most of the parking lots in downtown East St. Louis. He passed away quietly at age seventy-two in 1965, survived by his wife, daughter and granddaughter.

25

TODAY'S BOOKMAKERS

Today, bookmaking is becoming a part of the gaming establishment as a revenue source, just like East St. Louis mayor John T. Connors envisioned in the 1940s. Mayor Connors was on record that he didn't want to close down the bookmakers. He wanted to issue paying licenses for them to operate and create a revenue stream. Another benefit would be keeping workers employed in multiple spots.

Gambling has always been around, but now it is welcomed with open arms. The guards at the door frisking for weapons, staff walking among the crowd looking over things and pit bosses have been replaced in part by cameras, metal detectors, biometrics and other oversight of the funds flowing through the casinos. Casinos still bear a strong resemblance to past gambling, both legal and illegal, in the East Side and at the Ringside.

Gambling is now called gaming and encompasses a range of activities that reflects its popularity in the United States. Gaming in the country has evolved, beginning in East St. Louis and expanding to Las Vegas, then going from riverboat gambling to Atlantic City, to tribal council lands and to just about any place that can gain voter approval.

The latest iteration is the legalization of sports betting. This started with the May 2018 U.S. Supreme Court decision striking down an act stipulating that Nevada was the only place where sports betting was allowed. That act had been in effect for over twenty-five years. Any state could now allow sports betting if it was approved by its voters.

Today, bookies operate sports betting in a formal and legal environment in most states that have legalized the activity. Bookmakers now operate as a national business run by publicly listed companies. Some bookmakers are stand-alone operations; others are a part of a casino organization that also includes a sports book. In all cases, bets can be placed in person at a retail operation or online with a desktop or phone.

In 2020, the Casino Queen struck a deal with the sports bookmaker DraftKings to rebrand the property as DraftKings at Casino Queen. A $10 million renovation replaced and remodeled the restaurant and food choices and replaced the spaces with new facilities and a full sports book, which includes access to the DraftKings walk-up facility and its mobile betting app.

According to the *Wall Street Journal*, the sports betting market in the United States generated $7.9 billion in revenue in 2022. This was up from less than $1 billion in 2019. At the beginning of 2023, Ohio became the thirty-second state to legalize sports betting and recorded $11 million in transactions during its New Year's debut.

In 2023, the top bookmakers were considered to be the following: DraftKings, FanDuel, Bet MGM Sports Book, Caesars Sports Book, BetRivers, PointsBet, BetWay and FoxBet. The consensus is that only a few will survive, as large sums of money are being spent on advertising by a few and this will drive out smaller operations.

In contrast to the 1900–50 glory days of gambling, casinos and handbooks have become legal. Illinois began authorizing riverboat casinos in 1990 and became an early authorizer of sports betting. It began in June 2020 with Bet River, based in Chicago, followed by DraftKings and FanDuel in August 2020, PointsBet in September 2020, Barstool in March 2021, then Bet MGM and Caesars Sports Book in March 2022. License fees for the designated gaming operations fell in the $10 to $20 million range, one of the highest in the United States. The state also enjoys a percentage of the handle. In October 2022, Illinois posted its first $1 billion monthly sports wagering handle.

Fairmont Racetrack has joined with the sports betting firm FanDuel and is shown in a 2023 photo. *static. wixstatic.com/media.*

Football has taken over from the racehorses of Tom Shaw's days as the major choice of bettors. In 2023, you can walk up to the bookmaker at its physical location or make book online with your computer or phone. Sports betting is available for a wide variety of activities—basically, anything worth betting on. Bookmakers now offer bets and odds-on various combinations and outcomes, even during a game in progress.

The East Side is now referred to by a term encompassing a broader geographic area: the Metro East. The region now has legal bookmaking operations, in three locations, an echo of the days when there were three major bookmakers: Vic Doyle, Mulepole Fritz and Roy Bowman. Today's operations are in East St. Louis at the Casino Queen Hotel and Casino, with the bookmaker DraftKings; in Collinsville at the Fairmont Racetrack, with FanDuel Sports Book & Horse Racing; and to the north in Alton at the Argosy Casino, with Barstool.

The Casino Queen has rebranded, and there are now advertisements for bookies at a casino on the East Side. The Fairmont Park Racetrack has also joined the new wave, rebranding with the bookmaker FanDuel in its advertisements.

26

CURRENT OPERATIONS

Las Vegas essentially replaced East Side gambling. Bugsy Siegel's Flamingo began the exodus, and the Vegas Strip casinos continue to blossom today. Their monopoly has diminished somewhat, a result of all the new gaming laws and casinos now legally operating in the United States. Gaming is also prevalent in other countries and offers new opportunities. Macau, China, is the current favorite location for investment.

Even with all the changes, the Las Vegas Strip operations dominate the U.S. casino market. According to data from the American Gaming Association, excluding online sports betting or iGaming, total gaming revenue for the Las Vegas Strip market in 2022 amounted to approximately $8.2 billion. This made Vegas the number-one casino market. Number two was Atlantic City, with around $2.8 billion, and Baltimore–Washington, D.C., at number three with $2.175 billion. Chicago, Illinois–Indiana followed at $2.136 billion.

All of the betting kingpins profiled in this book recognized and tapped into the gambling popularity of their population base, which was extensive. That popularity continues to this day.

The East Side is now part of the St. Louis–area casino market (Missouri-Illinois). This ranked a robust number nine, at close to $1.1 billion in 2022. This market now includes Argosy Gaming, Casino Queen and Fairmont Racetrack, all with their own bookmakers. This market also includes casino operations in St. Louis's downtown with the Horseshoe. It is located on land but is near the Mississippi River and next to Eads Bridge. River City in South St. Louis County is also near the Mississippi. There is also Hollywood

Casino in West St. Louis County on the Missouri River and Ameristar on the Missouri River, just north of the Hollywood in downtown St. Charles. The State of Missouri has not passed legislation allowing sports betting at this time, nor have horse racetracks returned to the state.

Gaming thrives in the East Side, which has different sets of operations, players, methods, owners, regulations and formal legalization.

In addition to these markets, Native American tribes also have been operating casinos. New York State is influenced by Indian gaming locations in nearby Connecticut. Illinois and Missouri have no Indian gaming locations. The federal Indian Gaming Regulation Act was passed in 1988. It requires tribal and state governments to negotiate deals to operate casinos on tribal lands. According to figures from the National Indian Gaming Commission, tribal gambling revenue has grown from $121 million in 1988 to $39 billion for the 2021 fiscal year.

National and international corporations have taken over from organized crime. They have turned the gambling industry into an open multistate and international financial success for governments and publicly traded corporations. Independent gamblers can still be found, but nowhere to the extent of the era when the Ringside operated.

27

FUTURE DIRECTION

Mayor Connors's words have been realized. In 2024, the influence of gambling on a city's economy continues. Gambling has become a major selling point in providing a strong economic resource for community existence and development.

Today, the financial success of gaming continues. Commercial gambling revenues have surged, and signs indicate that this will continue. This has been especially pronounced with the legalization of walk-up and online sports betting and the number of states now approving their operation. Many states authorizing gambling now recognize the significant source of revenue that can be collected. States will become very protective of this revenue.

Native American tribes have felt left out in this new expansion of sports betting. According to the *Wall Street Journal*, the Bureau of Indian Affairs in 2022 proposed changes that would ease rules allowing tribes to acquire additional land for casino development and negotiate online-betting deals with states. The bureau cites as part of its responsibility to revitalize tribal communities by strengthening their homelands and economic self-sufficiency. The tribes recognize the influence of gambling on economic growth.

Amazingly, with all the changes in gambling, New York and Chicago do not have casinos within their boundaries. Gambling operations exist nearby, and it now looks like these cities will get their own.

In December 2022, Chicago gave building approval for its first casino. Plans call for Bally's to operate the venue. It is scheduled to be in a sector of the city's downtown area so it can stabilize and enhance additional economic development. The site is not far from Mont Tennes's 1910 operations. The city also views the casino as a major income source and stabilizer for its own financial challenges.

While no bookmakers were designated, it's a sure bet that the competition will be keen to be part of this operation. Its cost is estimated at $1.7 billion. It will include 3,400 slots, 173 table games, a five-hundred-room hotel, an exhibit area and eleven restaurants. Revenue is estimated at $800 million per year, and annual tax revenue going to the city is forecast in the $200 million range. Mont Tennes would be happy to see the action in his old neighborhood.

New York City and its central borough of Manhattan are also touting the potential of casinos to revitalize parts of that city. A series of proposals and sites are in discussion, with Caesars Entertainment Inc. as the designated operator, with sports betting. The company wants to be located in the Times Square area. Other groups are discussing midtown East Side locations, but with no designated casino operator as of this writing. The spirits of Honest John Kelly and Broadway Jack Doyle will be there to welcome the action.

28

REFLECTIONS

When putting these profiles together, I couldn't help but think of my dad, Ray Doyle.

He lived through most of these times and would have been elated to see the way sports betting has unfolded. He passed away in 1996, just shy of eighty-seven years old. He got to see a good portion of the changes to gaming. One thing he did just about every day in his later years was read the *Daily Racing Form*. He enjoyed handicapping the horses. He didn't bet on them anymore, but he liked to keep his mind alert, and handicapping was a pleasure he kept until shortly before his passing.

He and I were able to talk at length at times. Doing research on these profiles, I discovered that there were things that went beyond what he might have mentioned in passing.

He sort of skipped the real details about Uncle Vic being a kidnapping victim. Dad brought the ransom payoff to retrieve his brother. There are no further details and no reports to verify this, but it surely happened. He merely passed off any mention of the bombings at Uncle Vic's place, including their magnitude and frequency. And Mulepole Fritz's bombings were not discussed. Wortman's influence on Dad's change in life direction was never mentioned. But my dad sure made the point that he didn't want anything to do with Wortman or any of his associates. I could tell without knowing the true reason, but he said that Wortman and his group were people that you never wanted to have anything to do with.

Raymond Francis Doyle, the author's dad. He was a storyteller, World War II veteran, businessman and someone who lived his life as part of the greatest generation. *Doyle family photo, circa 1946.*

He mentioned Jimmy Carroll, but only talked about layoff bets and being at a hearing with him and Vic. Dad didn't mention Carroll's national prominence and testimony. It became clear to me in researching Carroll why Dad had our home TV turned to the Kefauver hearings. I don't remember Carroll, but I do remember hearing my sister say that she refused to answer any questions on grounds that it might incriminate her—constantly.

In thinking about putting these profiles together, I quickly became aware that the betting kingpins were all strong individuals who stood up to create personal and financial success. Helping others in need was always something my dad routinely tried to do for others, especially his older brothers.

Dad liked to read everything, not just the racing form. He read a variety of books, local and national newspapers, as well as magazines. He especially enjoyed following a select group of columnists. And he passed that on to me. One of his favorites was Damon Runyon of New York. In doing research for this book, I found that some of my profiles had been mentioned as characters in some Runyon columns. I figured if Damon looked at them in his day, they would be worthy of a look from a different time. I hope the readers of this book feel the same.

I originally started out on a project looking at my Uncle Vic and his Ringside place. It quickly expanded to other gamblers of his time and how things operated for them in the East Side. The scope and location shifted to other cities and to other kingpins comparable to Vic. The dominant players began to stand out. Those men I've chosen were picked because of what they first did as individuals, what they overcame and what they did to succeed. The obstacles were in many cases typical predicaments faced by business owners. In other cases, gaming and its political and legal status determined operational choices. These men's choices were made at the track or the casino or while looking at a handbook play out bookmaking probabilities.

The period between 1900 and 1950 was chosen for this to play out their probabilities due to the changing nature of gambling and the individuals participating. The year 1900 saw a number of states wanting to eliminate betting at its most popular form: horse racing. In 1950, the influence of organized crime was made apparent, as syndicates focused on gambling as a major income source. Anti-gambling sentiment was back in the picture. Throughout the fifty-year period, the independent, individual gambling operator was a major force. In 1900, the U.S. population was 76 million; by 1950, it had doubled, to over 150 million. By 2020, the nation's population had doubled again, to over 300 million. Gambling has remained through all of these population and economic changes. It has simply taken on different forms.

Today, gambling as seen as a major income source for governments, with organized crime out of the picture. The individual entrepreneurs featured in this book would be hard-pressed to exist at the same level in betting today. They would more likely be found at hedge funds. Big business has taken over the gaming industry. Kingpins looked not only at the betting odds; they also kept an eye on stock prices.

The national leaders in the gaming and bookmaking era of individual operators were concentrated in New York, Chicago and St. Louis. There were undoubtedly major players in other cities, like Atlantic City, Philadelphia, Detroit and Baltimore. San Francisco and Los Angeles played roles in the West, but not at the level they are today. The cities chosen for this profile were leaders on a national scale for most of this period. Of course, now Las Vegas ranks as top city in gambling. Organized criminals have disappeared from the scene there, and multinational corporations have taken over.

One thing stands out in the profiles featured in this book: family was important. I didn't find any loners. Barney and Mulepole didn't have children, but they had wives. The number of kingpins who had brothers stands out. My dad, Uncle Jim (whom I was named after) and Uncle Vic had a family operation. I didn't realize until my research that the kingpin I knew and met as Roy Bowman actually ran an operation for a time with his brother. This operation, though, was inherited from their father, also named Roy Bowman.

The Cella brothers kept their union going. Louis Cella had a vision of operating racetracks and kept to it no matter what the politicians in different states did. He brought his brother into the picture, and it turned out for the best. His brother Charlie's side of the family still owns and operates Oak Lawn Track in Hot Springs, Arkansas.

The Bidwill and Mara brothers are interesting when viewed together. Tim had children, two boys, and those brothers wound up running things. He gave up his lucrative bookmaking role for a money-losing sports team, but he picked a winner, and his boys ran things together for a while. One of the groups was bought out of his 50 percent interest; the other member is still operating the team with the son from a different family. The same happened with the Bidwills, with another 50 percent buyout of a brother, but the remaining grandson still has full control of his team.

Tom Shaw really stands out, not just by his size, but also by his winning place in New York society, especially with his son-in-law having a baseball stadium for the New York Mets named after him.

Men profiled here were immigrants from Germany, Russia and Mexico, like Barney, Mo and Concepion. The others were all first-born children of immigrants from Ireland, Italy and Germany. That would present itself somewhat differently today. There is now a much more diversified demographic and background of heritages.

It became clear that gambling provided an equal opportunity experience. In 1900, and before that, women were participants at the clubhouse for horse racing and placing bets. When possible, they were found participating at the casinos and used the handbooks. They gravitated to different choices in greater abundance than men, and the casinos were more than willing to accommodate their choices. That trend continues today.

Another thing I noticed while writing this book is that those profiled identified with their religion. Mo was Jewish; Catholicism was the dominant religion of the others. All the men were laid to rest with services of their chosen religions.

They put their faith into action when it came to some of the bets they made. Tom Shaw on several bets stood to lose millions of dollars. Chicago O'Brien had a pattern, and his level of bets even impressed Tim Mara for their size and wins. Tim didn't shrink in betting, either, with high dollar amounts for his day. It is a good thing he came out OK, allowing the football team to keep going. Jimmy Carroll's level of bets toward 1950 was unbelievable. If they didn't get laid off and he didn't secure a win on both sides, his life would have ended much earlier than it did.

This individual determination is still alive today. New businesses are being formed by aspiring kingpins. Their focus is not on odds-beating, as in Tom Kearney's days. They are looking for launch money, business creation, success, initial public offerings or buyouts. Then, in the vein of Elon Musk and Bernard Arnault, they look for new businesses to create or purchase.

Regardless of period, the kingpins all like the action.

BIBLIOGRAPHY

Newspapers

Belleville (IL) Daily Advocate. January 20, 1941; August 21, 1941; February 1, 1947; March 12, 1948; February 24, 1951; March 27, 1951.

Belleville (IL) News Democrat. February 20, 1947; March 1, 1950; February 24, 1951; May 1, 1951.

Boston Globe. January 5, 1900; March 27, 1904; February 24, 1936.

Brooklyn Daily Eagle. August 3, 1900; January 12, 1905; November 23, 1919; April 18, 1925; June 19, 1926; August 14, 1927; August 19, 1928; November 15, 1928; March 7, 1932; September 9, 1937.

Brooklyn Times Union. July 31, 1902; January 12, 1905; June 11, 1905; July 31, 1920; September 20, 1927; May 15, 1928; November 7, 1928; February 23, 1929; May 27, 1931; February 13, 1934; March 9, 1934; February 26, 1937.

Buffalo Courier. January 9, 1905; October 5, 1910; April 14, 1929.

Buffalo Express. October 22, 1905.

Buffalo Times. September 24, 1905; October 10, 1910.

Chicago Chronicle. March 18, 1877.

Chicago Tribune. January 20, 1901; October 1, 1903; October 25, 1903; August 1, 1904; December 21, 1906; October 3, 1907; October 5, 1907; December 27, 1908; November 8, 1909; December 21, 1909; December 31, 1909; October 4, 1911; October 14, 1911; November 18, 1911; April 4, 1914; August 1, 1914; September 21, 1920; November 2, 1924; January 23, 1925; February 1, 1925; February 17, 1925; September 24,

1926; October 18, 1930; January 4, 1935; October 18, 1936; July 22, 1937; March 29, 1951; May 29, 1951; April 29, 1993.

Cincinnati Inquirer. November 18, 1934.

Collyer's Eye (Chicago, IL). November 28, 1925; September 9, 1933; January 30, 1937.

Daily Advertiser (New Orleans). April 18, 1951.

Daily Missourian (Columbia, MO). March 10, 1917.

Daily Racing Form. September 1, 2006.

Daily Signal (New Orleans). January 8, 1916.

Decatur (IL) Herald. November 17, 1927.

Edwardsville (IL) Intelligencer. March 23, 1951.

Evening News (London, UK). March 20, 1927.

Evening World (New York). October 25, 1902.

Inter Ocean (Chicago, IL). June 2, 1903; July 6, 1903; August 9, 1906.

Jennings (Louisiana) Daily News. January 31, 1951; March 27, 1953; May 28, 1952.

Joliet (IL) Evening Herald. January 24, 1906; December 10, 1940.

Kansas City (MO) Star. August 3, 1925; January 19, 1930.

Kansas City (MO) Times. October 29, 1893; April 24, 1919; August 7, 1941.

Lexington (KY) Herald. November 4, 1928.

Los Angeles Times. August 22, 1951.

Messenger (Belleville, IL). December 14, 1936.

New York Daily News. November 16, 1925; March 5, 1926; June 5, 1930; February 18, 1931; March 10, 1932; March 22, 1932; January 22, 1933; November 6, 1936; February 19, 1938; August 7, 1941; January 22, 1950; January 18, 1994.

New York Herald. September 9, 1922.

New York Herald and Journal. November 4, 1936.

New York Tribune. October 11, 1918.

Pasadena (CA) Page. January 23, 1941.

Philadelphia Inquirer. December 1, 1899; June 27, 1934; June 21, 1940.

Pittsburgh Evening Express. May 12, 1925.

Pittsburgh Press. October 25, 1938; October 27, 1938; October 29, 1938.

Sandusky (OH) Register. October 3, 1939.

San Francisco Call. March 31, 1898.

Santa Anna (CA) Register. June 1, 1935.

Shreveport (LA) Journal. October 12, 1950.

Southern Illinoisan (Carbondale, IL). April 1, 1953.

Sportsman Review (Chicago, IL). April 13, 1904.

Star Tribune (Salt Lake City, UT). August 6, 1931, August 16, 1937.

St. Louis Globe-Democrat. August 2, 1858; December 24, 1892; December 28, 1903; February 8, 1920; November 29, 1934; April 5, 1935; February 24, 1936; October 16, 1936; January 30, 1937; June 17, 1941; September 30, 1941; March 4, 1951; October 12, 1952; June 3, 1955; January 12, 1960; October 9, 1960.

St. Louis Post-Dispatch. November 28, 1891; March 3, January 13, 1895; March 29, 1895; August 14, 1897; September 30, 1897; August 8, 1900; August 8, 1904; December 12, 1906; October 31, 1907; November 20, 1908; December 15, 1908; March 20, 1909; July 27, 1909; September 3, 1909; December 12, 1909; March 28, 1910; August 28, 1911; September 19, 1911; January 27, 1913; July 29, 1913; December 5, 1914; April 16, 1915; May 2, 1915; December 16, 1915; August 1, 1916; March 30, 1917; March 30, 1917; December 16, 1918; April 6, 1919; September, 19, 1919; September 24, 1919; November 4, 1920; August 8, 1927; January 7, 1930; April 17, 1932; January 24, 1934; December 5, 1938, November 3, 1940; June 18, 1944; April 22, 1947; August 9, 1950, January 2, 1951; February 25, 1951; July 17, 1953; February 16, 1967; June 1, 1971; January 18, 1992; September 26, 1982; April 29, 1994; June 22, 1997; September 10, 2022.

———. "Once-Forbidden Gambling Now Embraced By All." November 23, 2022.

St. Louis Republic. July 5, 1900.

St. Louis Star Times. November 21, 1919; September 6, 1923; January 23, 1925; February 25, 1930; August 30, 1935; December 16, 1946; April 22, 1947; April 25, 1947.

Sun (Baltimore, MD). February 6, 1913.

Times (Philadelphia). June 3, 1899.

Times (Shreveport, LA). March 29, 1951; September 26, 1956; January 19, 1957.

Wall Street Journal. November 26, 2022; December 1, 2022; December 20, 2022; January 26, 2023; February 16, 2023; March 20–21, 2023; March 16, 2023; March 30, 2023; April 24, 2023; April 17, 2023; April 22, 2023; April 29–30, 2023; May 8, 2023; May 11, 2023; May 19, 2023; June 8, 2023; June 10, 2023.

Books and Websites

American Gaming Association. "AGA Commercial Gaming Revenue Tracker." February 15, 2023. https://www.americangaming.org.

Ancestry.com. James R. Doyle Public Family Tree.

———. Thomas O'Brien Public Family Tree.

———. James O'Leary Public Family Tree.

———. Mont Tennes Public Family Tree.

Chavdar. "History of Gambling in the US: A Timeline." Play Today. October 27, 2023. https://playtoday.co.

East St. Louis Research Project. "East St. Louis Police." http://www.eslarp.uiuc.edu.

Lawrence, Christina, and Kathryn O'Dwyer, eds. "'Tolerating' Gambling." New Orleans Historical. www.neworleanshistorical.org.

Legal Betting. "States with Horse Betting." https://www.legalbetting.com.

May, Allan. "The History of the Race Wire Service, Part II." Crime Magazine. https://www.crimemagazine.com.

Mooney, Katherine C. *Isaac Murphy*. New Haven, CT: Yale University Press, 2023.

Newspapers.com.

Sports Handbook. December 2022. www.sportshandbook.com.

Thompson, Marissa. "A Brief History of Gambling in the United States." Communities for Positive Youth Development. December 3, 2020. https://www.cpydcoalition.org.

Wikipedia. "Argosy Gaming Company." https://en.wikipedia.org.

———. "Casino Queen." https://en.wikipedia.org.

———. "Daily Racing Form." https://en.wikipedia.org.

———. "Fairground Park Media/File St. Louis Fairgrounds." https://en.wikipedia.org.

———. "Fairgrounds Racecourse New Orleans." https://en.wikipedia.org.

———. "Gambling in State of New Jersey." https://en.wikipedia.org.

———. "Harrah's New Orleans." https://en.wikipedia.org.

———. "Louis Cella." https://en.wikipedia.org.

———. "United States Senate Special Committee to Investigate Crime in Interstate Crime in Interstate Commerce." https://en.wikipedia.org.

ABOUT THE AUTHOR

James R. Doyle is founder of St. Louis–based James R. Doyle Incorporated, which has delivered professional services to a national client base. He created and served as editor/publisher of the firm's banking publications, as well as author and project director for several contracted economic and land-development studies. His present focus is on historical research dealing with social and economic changes that have impacted communities across the United States.